BLOCKCHAIN, CRYPTOCURRENCIES & THE FUTURE

This book will help you to understand the new and emerging world of blockchain and cryptocurrencies from an Australian layman's perspective.

There is a common belief in the public that cryptocurrency is 'everything one does not understand about money combined with everything one does not understand about computers'.

Brian McNicol

Muthu Pannirselvam

Disclaimer

The information contained in this book is given in good faith and has been derived from sources believed to be accurate at the time of writing. No liability will be accepted by the authors or publishers for actions taken by any person on the strength of this information alone. It is recommended that professional independent advice be sought.

First published in February 2019 by Arthur Phillip Books

Cover designed by Brian McNicol and Muthu Pannirselvam

Book formatting by *Grand Park Australia*

Table of Contents

A word from author Brian McNicol

Both Muthu and I were intrigued by the euphoria surrounding Bitcoin and the talk of a Bubble in particular in the later part of 2017. Almost overnight 'experts' emerged selling expensive educational programs. (That maybe an exaggeration as they appeared to be expensive newsletters). In December 2018, we don't know of any of these educational programs still being promoted.

Our attention was further heightened when John Lindeman, a respected property market analyst in Australia, produced some interesting comparisons between the rise of Bitcoin and the Wall Street stock market crash of 1929 and, more recently, the housing market crash in the mining regions such as Moranbah in 2013.

Following one of Warren Buffet's sayings, *'I read and think. So, I do more reading and thinking and make less impulse decisions than most other people in business'*. Maybe this is what people buying cryptocurrency should have done ? Also remember Warren Buffett's other rule – *'Rule No 1 Never lose money, Rule No 2, never forget Rule No 1'*. We could see the herd mentality appearing as we had seen in the mining towns in Queensland and Western Australia. Before any consideration of investing, we wanted to know more detail as the education courses didn't appear to provide the information we wanted and other sources didn't appear objective. So we started reading what we could, mainly blogs, and found no books that were written for the Australian market.

This book has been written by two novices for people seeking to learn about blockchain and cryptocurrencies like Bitcoin.

It was written by Australians for the Australian market although much of the content is universal. For the Australian market, we have included chapters on superannuation and taxation.

From the sale of any of our books, we have undertaken to support two very special and worthwhile charities ......

Firstly, the *Destiny Rescue*, an Australian initiative that is touching many lives across the world. *Destiny Rescue* is a non-profit organisation that is striving hard to end child sexual exploitation and slavery. Secondly, *Opportunity International* exists to bring about a measure of justice, dignity and purpose for families living in poverty. They do this by supporting local microfinance organisations that provide innovative financial solutions to empower people, create small businesses and build vibrant communities.

Please discourage any form of illegal downloads of this book that defeats the purpose of the series published by Arthur Phillip Books. We wish you the best of luck on your property journey and may your dreams come true in the near and the distant future!

Visit our website for recent updates, blogs and other interesting information on properties: *arthurphillipbooks.com*

Acknowledgements

We would like to acknowledge the valuable knowledge and assistance provided by the following;

Nagarajan Kuppuswamy, *Oracle India*

A full stack developer, *Belgium*

A Blockchain Consultant, *Blockchain Centre, Australia*

Dr Hemachander Subramanian, *Moffitt Cancer Center, Florida*

Ganesh Rajagopalan, IT Consultant, *San Francisco*

And Tony Skinner, our long-suffering but most-valued editor.

The input that each has contributed in their area of expertise been invaluable and greatly appreciated. Without their contributions, it is unlikely that this book would be as detailed and current as it is.

Preface

In 1776, the free world's first economist, Adam Smith, envisaged a world of free markets and global trade in his book "*The Wealth of Nations*". These free trade markets have lifted many millions of people out of poverty but have also introduced various regulations. We live in a free world where we choose what we want to do, providing we abide by various rules and regulations. The internet has crept in and some would say has taken over our lives.

A free market opens our minds to new and revolutionary ideas and it helps us to be more productive and more skilful with limited resources. In his *Wealth of Nations*, Adam Smith mentioned that the market has to be practical, open-minded and not shackled to any pre-existing ideology.

Economic progress in the past few centuries, right from the first industrial revolution, has been explosive and exponential; however the world has seen economic depression, inflation, stagflation and much more.

The globalisation has brought unprecedented prosperity but also brought crisis and risk that we are only beginning to understand in the past few decades. Producing where it is most effective, selling where it is more profitable, and sourcing where it is cheapest without worrying about national boundaries, is the fundamental principle of globalisation. Due to the globalisation and free market, the flow of investments, ideas, business and culture has happened very quickly. While there are risks associated with globalisation, there is no alternative to it.

In 2008, the financial markets went into freefall across the world. The global financial crisis (GFC) was a combination of many mistakes in various countries. It resulted in some governments going broke; many people lost jobs, their lifetime savings and much more. The global recessions costs tens of trillions of dollars, 30 million people lost their jobs and it increased the national debt for many countries.

However, during the time of this global financial crisis, one person saw an opportunity and introduced blockchain and Bitcoin. Neither created a great deal of publicity at that time; it is only in the last few years that people are talking about blockchain and Bitcoin.

Now with all the current euphoria and volatility around one cryptocurrency (namely Bitcoin), we are intrigued by Bitcoin and the origins of cryptocurrencies. We are also amazed that not everyone has heard of Bitcoin and that, of those that have, only a very small fraction understand it. People are being encouraged, maybe by fear of missing out, to place their money into an 'investment' that many don't understand on the expectation that their money will have a meteoric rise in value.

With little knowledge of blockchain or any of the cryptocurrencies, we set out to write a book that explains, in simple terms, what is Bitcoin and other cryptocurrencies, what the blockchain is and how they are related. We wanted to write a book that anyone could read and understand. This technology, in the near future, is likely to revolutionise our world just as computers and the internet have done in recent history.

We wanted to look at whether there is a *Bitcoin Bubble* as some people speculated, and what we can learn, if anything, from history. In mid-2017, the value of many of these cryptocurrencies climbed dramatically but in December 2017, a dramatic fall for Bitcoin resulted in a loss of about 40 percent of its value in just under a week. $19,796 per Bitcoin on 17 December plummeted to $11,590 on 22 December, according to *Coinbase*. On the 21 December 2018, Bitcoin was priced at $5,666. Yes, we hear the 'cryptonerds' saying that they have still made money and, yes, they have if they purchased a Bitcoin for less than $5,666 or less and the price drops further. Yes, in all likelihood, Bitcoin will go back up – but do people want a currency that has such spectacular booms and busts?

Bitcoin has spawned various opportunities in areas such as multi-level marketing and education. Unfortunately, it appears that, like the developer of Bitcoin, secrecy abounds with cryptocurrencies. From the education courses and multi-level marketing that we looked at, a new wave of experts were offering their recently discovered expertise. Many experts were promoting 'follow these instructions' and, as some refer to it, 'place your bet and do not risk any more than you can afford to lose'. Some of these cryptocurrency experts were, only 12 months or so ago, on the educational circuits promoting property, shares or Forex trading.

Is Bitcoin and other cryptocurrencies a legitimate step forward towards a cashless society?

At the present time, neither of the authors own, nor have owned, any cryptocurrencies. We are not involved in any way with education, selling or endorsing any cryptocurrency. We are amazed at the hysteria that Bitcoin and other cryptocurrencies can generate on the various forums that we have looked at in our research.

The aim of this book is to look at the history of cryptocurrencies, (and Bitcoin in particular), what other comparable products are in the market place, and to compare these with historical events such as the tulip mania in the 1636, *Poseidon* in the 1970s and more recently the *Dotcom bubble* around 1997 to 2001.

Some have described cryptocurrency as an underground banking system or, as one described Bitcoin, 'a market for criminals and millennials'. This seems a somewhat harsh assessment. We will look at what may happen if there is a rush of people wanting to convert their cryptocurrency to traditional currency like US or Australian dollars, euro or pound sterling.

We will look at what roles governments play both in Australia and around the world, and the possible effects on the banking system as we know it.

We will look at how cryptocurrency and blockchain are intertwined. But to be fair to blockchain and others like it that are following, we have devoted distinct chapters to blockchain.

Finally, we will look at cryptocurrency as an investment for Self-Managed Superannuation Funds (SMSFs) and the various tax implications for cryptocurrencies in Australia.

We offer no opinion as to whether cryptocurrency is good or bad and, at most, we may sound a word of caution based on history. Yes, there may be a lot of money to be made from cryptocurrencies and some people with a little knowledge and a few years' experience are already making money in the 'education' arena.

It remains to be seen whether Bitcoin or any of the *Altcoins* will take over as a universal currency, whether any of the cryptocurrencies will take over as a replacement for gold in times of economic uncertainty, or whether any of the other claims made by the proponents of the cryptocurrency will eventuate.

Blockchain certainly has advantages and many applications across a whole spectrum of economic activities so this area will continue to develop and expand.

There is a lot of detail to become familiar with in the emerging world of blockchain and cryptocurrencies. Developments and changes will continue.

The information in this book should not be interpreted as an endorsement of any cryptocurrencies or a recommendation to invest in any cryptocurrencies. As with other investments, historic performance is no guarantee of future returns. As an investment class, cryptocurrencies are highly speculative investments and investing in cryptocurrencies involves significant risks – they are highly volatile, vulnerable to hacking and capital loss, and sensitive to secondary activity. Before investing you should obtain sound independent advice and decide whether the potential return outweighs the risks. Any investment should be a small part of your overall investment plan.

1   A Brief History of Money

Down through the ages, mankind has had a need to trade. With trade the barter system developed. As trade developed across countries, money developed. Money, whether shells, coins, skins or paper has no value apart from the value that people place on it. Money's value is derived from it being a medium of exchange, a unit of measurement or to store wealth. The value of money is due to the fact that everyone knows it is accepted as a form of payment. Aristotle, the Greek philosopher contemplated money in about 350BCE. According to Aristotle, every object has two uses: the original purpose for which it was designed, grown or made and secondly as an item to trade. Throughout the history of bartering or money, the underlying requirement has been trust. Trust in the person you deal with and trust that the medium of exchange will still be worth at least what you paid for it.

In this chapter we will look at how money has developed over the centuries from the early barter system to the start of cryptocurrencies.

Money in the form of coins is relatively new. In the very beginning, a barter system developed most likely in local areas and then became more widespread, even internationally. Barter is simply any exchange of goods, resources or services for mutual benefit.

From around 9000 BC, cattle, sheep, camels and other livestock were used to barter. When agriculture flourished and more grains, vegetables and other plant products were produced surplus to the requirements of the family or tribe, then these also were used for bartering with other families or tribes who lacked these goods. Other commodities like salt and weapons have also been traded over time. Bartering was first recorded in Egypt.

Historically many societies have used shells such as the *Cowrie* shell and its first use was around 1200 BC in China. The Cowrie shell has been the longest and most widely used shell, used until the middle of the last century in some parts of Africa. In the 14th century, the North American Indians used *wampum*, strings of white beads made from clam shells as a means of exchange.

The barter system worked for items with the greatest utility and reliability in terms of re-use and re-trading and for those goods bought out of necessity.

Bartering had some disadvantages. A barter cannot proceed until agreement is reached and some people may have felt lacking in their negotiating skills. Also, taking the livestock or produce with them to trade was time consuming and cumbersome and depended on a coincidence of wants.

Recalling the childhood story of *Jack and the Beanstalk*, Jack and his mother are in difficult times and decide that they have to sell their old cow to buy seed to plant a crop. As the story goes, Jack meets a man who offers to sell Jack magic beans. Jack is happy after receiving a reassurance that he would get his old cow back if the beans weren't magic. In this simple example, Jack is prepared to give his cow to the man in exchange for the magic beans and the man is prepared to accept the cow as payment for the magic beans.

Reality is a little more complicated as the seller has to find someone who wants to buy and then that buyer has to be able to offer the seller something that is wanted in exchange for the goods or services. As with Jack offering his old cow for magic beans, there is no agreed standard measure. Is a cow worth more, less or the same as a magic bean? It depends on the two parties.

First recorded around 3000 BC, the Mesopotamian civilisation developed the *shekel* which was both a unit of weight and currency and referred to a specific weight of barley being equivalent to a certain amount of silver, bronze or copper. The Egyptians used gold bars of a set weight as a medium of exchange.

Around 1000 BC, at the end of the Stone Age, China manufactured imitation cowrie in both copper and bronze. China also developed miniature replicas of tools such as daggers, hoes and spade. Practicality possibly played a part in the next stage as China developed a primitive version of the round coin. These coins, made out of base metal, contained a hole enabling coins to be held together like a chain. Coins also appeared separately in India (punched metal disks) and the cities around the Aegean Sea (heated and hammered with insignia) between 700 BC and 500 BC.

Sometime between 600 BC and 500 BC, the first coins were developed in Lydia, now part of present-day Turkey, by *King Alyattes*. They were developed using electrum, a naturally occurring mix of silver and gold that, in order to mark their authenticity and denominations, were stamped with images of various gods and emperors. The first coin featured a roaring lion. This currency helped increase both internal and external trade resulting in Lydia becoming one of the richest empires in Asia Minor.

This new coinage was copied by the Greeks, Persians, Macedonians and Romans, and refined as it was developed. Unlike the base metal used by China, silver, bronze and gold were used by other countries. These coins allowed trade to flourish around the Mediterranean Sea.

The next development occurred around 118 BC, again in China, when a one-foot square of white deerskin with colourful borders was used as money. This leather money is considered the first documented type of banknote and would have been lighter and easier to carry than a lot of coins.

Some of our sayings have come about through the history of money. For example, the phrase 'to pay through the nose' came from Ireland. Around 800 BC to AD 900, if anyone failed to pay the Danish poll tax in Ireland, the Danes would slit the nose of the offender.

Circa AD 806, the first known paper money appeared in China and was used for about 600 years and, in 1455, paper money disappeared from use in China. Like many countries today, China produced more and more paper notes until the value of the notes depreciated and inflation soared.

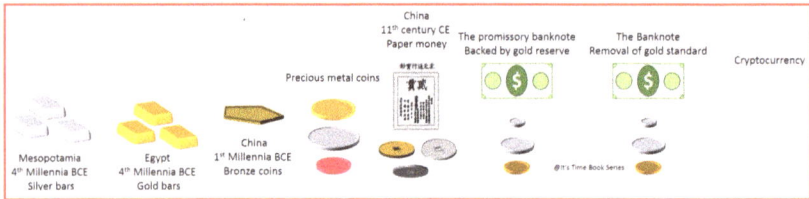

Figure 1: **History of money since 4th Millennium BC**

Traders and adventurers like Marco Polo in AD 1200 would have seen, and no doubt recounted, China's use of paper money and various denominations when they returned to Europe. Europeans continued to use coins as there was a plentiful supply of precious metals coming back from overseas colonies. In AD1250, a gold coin was printed in Florence, Italy. The *florin* was widely accepted across Europe and international commerce flourished. Money increased the speed at which business could be done.

Practicalities of trade and transferring larger sums of money around and between countries saw banks using bank notes for depositors and borrowers. These bank notes were issued by individual banks and could be exchanged at that bank for their face value in silver or gold coins. The first bank note was printed in Sweden in 1661.

The shift from coins to paper money in England and Europe increased international trade, resulting in banks and the rich ruling-class buying and receiving currencies from other nations. This in turn gave rise to the first currency exchange.

The value of a country's currency was influenced by the stability of a particular monarchy or government and how well it responded to currency wars between countries.

The next important event in the development of money was in 1816 when England made gold the standard of value. Bank notes had been used in Europe and England for hundreds of years before but the value of these notes was not tied to anything. Now, the bank notes became tied to gold. Guidelines were put into place to allow for the non-inflationary production of standard banknotes representing a certain amount of gold. America followed in 1900 with the *Gold Standard Act* which helped establish a central bank.

The *United States of America* (USA) government had raised money in preparation for World War 1 through raising taxes and selling *Liberty Bonds*. By 1914, the USA possessed an abundance of money in the form of gold but paper money was scarce. The USA was able to send large amounts of gold across the Atlantic to Britain. From this point, the US dollar became the preferred currency by exporters and the standard for international trade.

But the gold standard was short-lived as a result of the Great Depression.

In 1944, the *United Nations Monetary and Financial Council* adopted the *Bretton Woods* system which tore apart the gold standard and saw the US dollar linked to gold and the rest of the world linked their currency to the US dollar.

In the mid-to-late 20th century, the form of money was again changing. The first credit card was introduced in 1946 and the 1950s saw the introduction of the *Diners Club* card and the *American Express* card.

In 1971, former president *Richard Nixon* announced the temporary suspension of the convertibility of dollars to gold or other reserve assets and introduced a system of national *fiat* money – the beginning of the end for money backed by gold. This gives rise to fiat currency that has no intrinsic value. The central authority or federal reserve in each country has the right to control the currency flow in a market by raising interest rates (to slow down the economy), printing more money (to kick start an economy) and so forth. When government creates more money to kick-start the economy, the existing money already in the market loses its value. This process of limited and unlimited cashflow, controlled by a central authority, has directly impacted local and global economy many times since the Great Depression.

In 1974, *Bankcard* was introduced to Australia and, in the 1980's, *Visa* and *Mastercard* followed, allowing international usability.

Coins and bank notes remain but plastic debit and credit cards are reducing the needs for physical money. Smartphones allow people to pay for goods and services at the point of sale with 'tap and go'. But we have also seen the return to the barter system, the process being streamlined by such systems as *Bartercard*.

Credit card type products were invented in the early 1950s, well before the concept of internet technology. The latter has swept the world off its feet for the past 15 years but we still use 1950s technology (credit card) in conjunction with the internet.

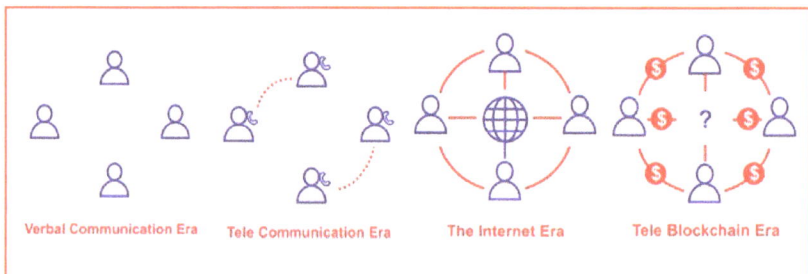

Figure 2: Right place/right time/right technology where humans are more connected than ever before (transition from verbal, telecommunication, internet, Teleblockchain)

The security features of transactions, including credit cards, had to be modified eventually to suit internet applications. Credit card set its foundation among customers to spend money without physically touching the money in all transactions. Credit cards also encouraged customers to live on borrowed money.

For many countries, the cashless society has arrived but, for many third-world countries, there are still no proper banking structures or, at best, poor banking supervision and unorthodox practices.

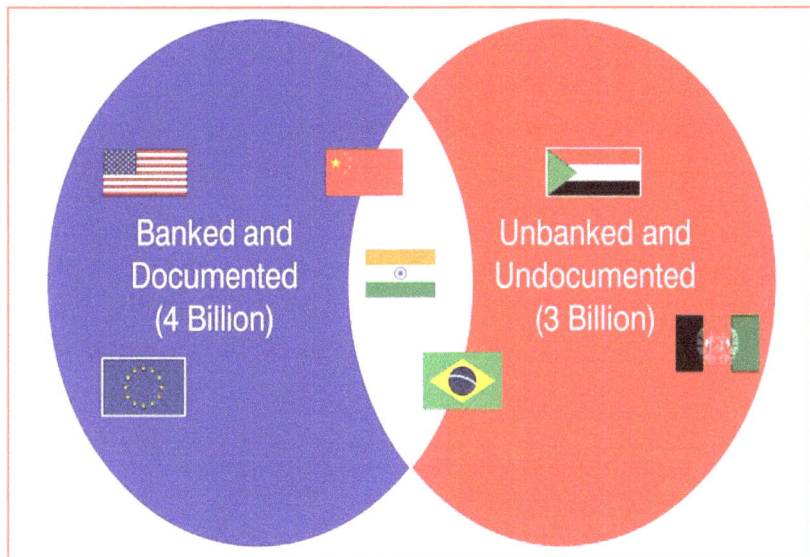

Figure 3: **Venn diagram showing the world population of banked & documented and unbanked & undocumented population**

In 2009, Bitcoin and virtual currencies arrived with claims that traditional notes and coins issued by governments were doomed as were centralised banks and their high transaction fees. Virtual currencies have no physical coinage and, to date, there is no standout cryptocurrency that is likely to be a world currency.

Today, in the digital age, we have wearable technology such as the *Barclaycard*, which is trialling contactless payment wristbands, and a microchip insertion under the skin. Money, in whatever form, has no intrinsic value. Whether it be a shell, precious coins, paper bank notes or cryptocurrencies, it is nothing apart from the value that people place on it. It has nothing to do with the physical value of money. Money allows people to trade goods and services, understand the price of these goods and services and allows money owners to plan and save for larger purchases such as a car or a house in the future. The value of money lies in the fact that other people will accept it as a form of payment.

It is often misunderstood that the greatest trade across borders around the world is not products and goods moving across the borders but **money**. There is a continuous flow of bonds, stocks, currencies, pension funds and so on. The annual trade in goods and services accounts for eight trillion dollars globally whereas trade in currencies accounts for 288 trillion dollars annually.

Money, as we have seen, has not always been a medium of exchange but it has become the backbone of each country's economy. Unfortunately, in today's society with the internet connecting the world, our present system of money exchange is not keeping pace with other technologies.

Australia's brief history of money

Like other civilisations, the Australian Aboriginal used a barter system to trade between neighbouring language groups as well as over vast distances.

Unlike those in other areas like Egypt and the Middle East where food and livestock were traded, these were not traded by the Aboriginals. Stones for implements, ochres, spinifex gum, ceremonial items and other resources not available in their tribal area were traded. The stems and leaves of the Pituri which grows in south-western Queensland and Central Australia were traded over an area of about 500,000 square kilometres. The plant contains nicotine and is psychotropic but, when mixed with alkaline wood ash, it was used as a tobacco, as a stimulant on long journeys and in ceremonies. Trade routes followed dreaming trials and it appears that goods may have changed hands a number of times through a number of language groups and cultural regions. Trade for Aboriginal people was more than physical items; it also included songs, dance, art, stories, rituals and ceremonies.

As in Europe, there is evidence of Aboriginals having market places where they would meet to exchange goods. From the time of European settlement in 1788, the Aboriginal trade routes were disrupted when settlements were established and fences for cattle and sheep were constructed.

Australia had been settled as a penal colony so it was thought, by the English Parliament, that no currency was required. The little currency that was available came from the officers and sailors and was a mix of English coins, guilders, ducats, rupees, Johannes, mohurs and Spanish dollars. However, the distance from England meant that notes and coins were in very short supply and disagreement about the value of each coin was common. In 1800, Governor King issued a *Currency Proclamation* establishing each coin's official value. In the same year, the *Cartwheel Penny* became Australia's first coin when it was exported to New South Wales from England. Governor King's Currency Proclamation placed a higher value on this coin than its face value in an attempt to keep them in the colony.

A complex barter system had also developed among the settlers. Food, clothing and alcohol were only available for the wealthy free settlers, merchants or high ranked military. Rather than being paid in money, convicts and lower military ranks were paid in goods such as food, clothing and the most popular: rum. Rum was the unofficial currency for the first 25 years of settlement.

Coinage remained in short supply as the colony expanded and, in an attempt to overcome the shortage, Governor Macquarie imported 40,000 Spanish dollars. These became the *Holey Dollar and Dump* in 1813 when William Henshall, a convicted forger, removed the central plug from the Spanish dollar to create two coins. The Holey dollar was given the value of five shillings and the dump one shilling and three pence.

Settlers had moved to South Australia and there was still an urgent need for currency so The *Adelaide Pound* was made in

1852 using gold from the Victorian goldfields. This coin was issued without approval from Britain so it was technically illegal but still widely accepted in the colony.

The colonies were given permission to open the first mint in Sydney in 1853 and the first Australian sovereign was produced in 1855 but not declared legal tender (including in Britain) until 1866. Other mints opened in Melbourne and Perth in 1872 and 1899 respectively.

Following the proclamation of the Commonwealth of Australia in 1901, Australia's first coins – florin, shilling, sixpence and threepence – were issued in 1910 and, in 1911, the first penny and half penny. In 1965, the first mint in Australia which was not a branch of the Royal Mint in London was established in Canberra. It produced Australia's decimal notes and coins released on 14 February 1966. In 1988 Australia introduced the first polymer note and, in that year, replaced the two dollar note with the two-dollar coin. Four years prior Australia had replaced the one-dollar note with a coin.

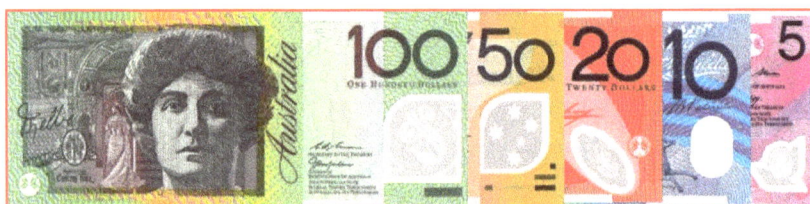

Figure 4: **Image showing Australian banknotes ($5, $10, $20, $50 and $100 notes)**

Today, the Australian dollar is the fifth most traded currency in the world. It is popular among traders because of the high interest rates in Australia, the stability of the economy and political system, and the lack of intervention by a central bank.

Numbers

Numbers are the fundamental driving force behind any engineering, technology or computer-aided project. Philosophy and decision making can be simplified through mathematics by viewing complex things through a simple set of equations. People like the decimal number system because it seems 'natural' in the same way they learned to count on their fingers. The base number is always greater than 1. The base for decimal is 10, for binary it is 2, for octal it is 8 and for hexadecimal it is 16. The higher the base, the easier it is to represent in a smaller way.

Prime numbers

The prime numbers were hardly used until the 1970s. Prime numbers are divisible only by 1 and by itself. Mathematicians used the prime numbers to encode and decode messages. In the 1970s, they came up with the idea of public key encryption. Public key encryption is a method whereby anyone can encode a message but only those people (who know the key) can decode the message.

Binary system

Binary digits (or bits) are an ingenious means of representing numerals. The processes use a combination of two symbols, 0 and 1. The two states (0 or 1) are like north-south in a magnetic field, open or closed in a relay switch, yes/no, or on/off.

In the days of pre-electronic machines and mechanical hand-driven calculators, gear wheels operated the mechanisms. It was challenging to grind ten teeth accurately and equi-distant. Binary (0 or 1) was chosen as a better alternative.

The most common and generally adopted numbering system is based on 10 (0,1,2...8,9). All computer languages and programming are based on the 2-digit number. Computers take the data and represent it as 0 and 1. This process is called digital encoding.

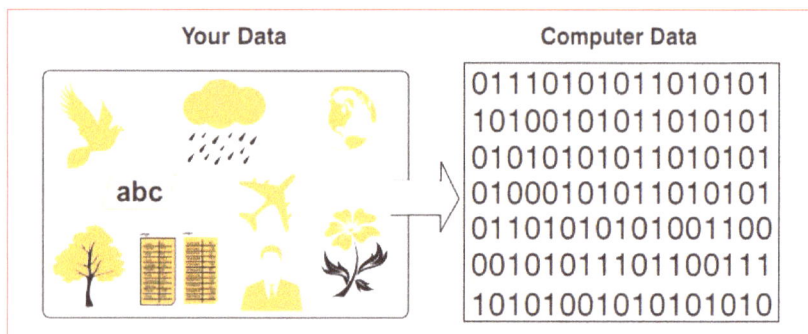

Figure 5: **Correlation of all the data collected daily and transferred to binary digits (computer data)**

Every computer is based on micro-transistors which make up the microprocessor. Transistors are designed with two stable states, yes or no, on or off, 0 or 1. The 0 and 1 are the only two binary digits and are often referred to as 'bits', also called 'binary digits'. A byte is 8 of these bits in a row. A binary number is called base 2. The bits in a binary number have position values '2 power 0', '2 power 1', '2 power 2'... 2 power n

Table 1: Numbers in decimal and binary system	
Decimal (base 10)	Binary (base 2)
0	0
1	1
2	10
3	11
4	100
5	101
6	110
7	111
8	1000
9	1001
10	1010
11	1011
12	1100
43	101011
50	110010
100	1100100
512	1000000000

Figure 6: Microtransistors off (0) and on (1)

Figure 7: Microtransistors converting data into computer recognised binary data (the above transistors pattern is equivalent to number 43)

2 Cryptography

The aim of cryptography is to make a message so scrambled that the original message cannot be read by a third party. The encrypted messages are understood only by people who are expected to know what the messages mean. The solution to understanding the hidden message is called 'the key'.

The main functions are:

1. Confidentiality – information is only accessible by a person(s) authorised to access it
2. Authentication – the receiver of a message knows who sent the message
3. Integrity – the receiver of a message is able to verify that the message has not been modified in transit
4. Non-repudiation – the sender should not be able to falsely deny that they sent the message

There is a similarity between physical and cipher locks: the key. In the case of a physical lock, when person A locks their message in a box and sends the key to person B, the key is available to only A and B and the message can be read by only A or B.

Figure 8: Physical lock (combination) vs cipher lock (password)

In terms of a cipher lock, person A encrypts (locks) the message using a combination of algorithms or mathematical functions. Person B receives the message with the code (shared in advance by person A). This process of opening the lock using a code is called decryption.

Encryption (Encoding) and Decryption (Decoding)

Encryption is a process of taking a message and scrambling its contents so that only certain people understand that message. Decryption (decoding) is the process of revealing the message.

With a single key, the words can be made to look gibberish but it contains a hidden meaning. Below is an example of a simple substitution cipher (mono-alphabetic) whereby each character in the plain text is replaced with a corresponding character of cipher-text. Underneath the encryption layer there is still a plain text that can be used by any attacker in an attempt to steal the encryption key for such password. Users remember the password (aw3somepassw0rd) as plain texts (an alphanumeric combination).

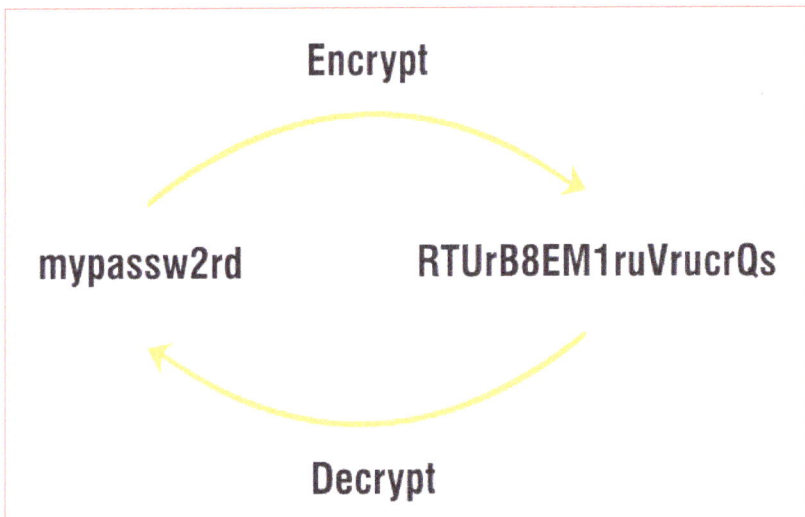

Encrypt

mypassw2rd   **RTUrB8EM1ruVrucrQs**

Decrypt

Figure 9: **The process of encryption and decryption**

Another example of encoding (encryption) and decoding (decryption) is as follows. The words "Arthur Phillip Books" can be scrambled in various forms using the following secret decoder.

	Word 1	Word 2	Word 3
With no encryption	ARTHUR	PHILLIP	BOOKS
D,4	XOQERO	MEFIIFM	YLLHP
H,4	TKMANK	IABEEBI	UHHAI
R,24	DUWKXU	SKLOOLS	ERRNV

Figure 10: **Decoder with various settings**

Table 2: The words "Arthur Phillip Books" after using the decoder (D4, H4, R24)			
	Word 1	**Word 2**	**Word 3**
With no encryption	ARTHUR	PHILLIP	BOOKS
D,4	XOQERO	MEFIIFM	YLLHP
H,4	TKMANK	IABEEBI	UHHAI
R,24	DUWKXU	SKLOOLS	ERRNV

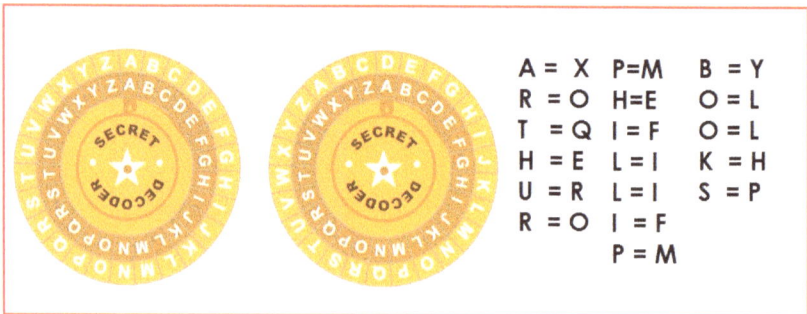

A = X	P=M	B = Y
R = O	H=E	O = L
T = Q	I = F	O = L
H = E	L = I	K = H
U = R	L = I	S = P
R = O	I = F	
	P = M	

Figure 11: **Decoder with D,4 key code**

In this case, D,4, Arthur Phillip Books can be encoded as listed on the table. The sender or receiver that has access to the code could only encode or decode the message. When the sender is encoding the message, letters from the inner wheel are matched with the letters on the outer wheel. When the receiver is decoding the message into the code, letters from the outer wheel are matched with the letters on the inner wheel. An interceptor that received the code "XOQERO MEFIIM YLLHP" would not be able to interpret the message until they knew the key code. In the above decoder, the sender can spin the wheel further, if needed, to make it more complex. This encoding can be fast-tracked to create multiple alphanumeric digits using advanced computers. An advanced computer with a modern graphical processing unit can process up to 290 million digits per second. (See also *Hashing* for more details).

In an encryption process, there are two keys: public keys and private keys. A public key can be given to anyone, the other key must be kept private.

In cryptocurrency and blockchain, there are also public and private keys.

Public key and private key

A public key can be compared to a mailbox in a street. The address is known to everyone but the key to open the mail box is a private key. The owner of that mailbox can only open it with a private key.

Figure 12: **Depiction of a mailbox to explain public key and private key**

Table 3: Difference between public key and private key	
Public key	**Private key**
Location of the mailbox in front of a property: street number, street name, suburb, country, and postcode are like the public key (known to everyone)	The key that belongs to the owner of the mail box is like a private key.

Cryptography history

The very first encryption of messages was used during Roman Empire called *Caesar Cypher*.

Recent history has brought cryptography to the public eye…….

During World War 2, the Germans encrypted their messages using a machine called *Enigma*. The enigma (encrypted) messages were used for all major communications. The location of every U-boat, location of secret convoys and other details were fed into an enigma machine. The message sent from an enigma machine was completely gibberish unless the reader had an encryption key to decode the information.

All the messages were travelling through the air via radio waves. The radio signals could be intercepted by AM signals but the messages were encrypted and breaking the codes manually would have taken years. Processing time and speed became key factors for survival in war. This gave rise to the origin of computers (to compute faster) because the Allies found it very hard to break with manual techniques.

Using another machine named *Bombe* built at Bletchley radio manufacturing company in the UK, the Allies managed to break the enigma code and shortened World War II by two years. This saved millions of lives.

Since the end of the *Cold War*, a lot of former physicists, mathematicians and statisticians have applied their knowledge and skills, not on cold war technology, but to economics and financial markets. Some of the developments in the financial markets also include: credit default swap, derivatives, cryptocurrencies, blockchain mechanism and so on. There are a few concepts that have become destructive to us globally; for example complex financial products like derivatives and credit default swap. These were the major factors in the economic turmoil in 2008. The finance industries employed people to work on destructive applications.

Computers

Numbers are an integral part of our lives; humans have always attempted to ease the burden of computation. In cryptocurrency, mining is the process of running complicated computations in the search for a specific number. The *abacus* was an early method of calculation and is still used today. The slide rule, electronic calculator and then the microcomputer evolved with advancements in technology.

The first computing machine, invented by Charles Babbage, was a mechanically-driven computer vastly different to the computers of today which use an integrated chip (IC). The impact of computers is extensive with applications ranging from complex computations to a simple air conditioning control. These applications are constantly evolving as we create more and more accessories to make the computer perform better. The performance of any computer depends on how well the parts of a computer – mother board, central processing unit, memory, hard disk, video card, graphics card, graphics processing unit – are assembled by the manufacturers.

Computers work faster as the microprocessor speed increases. The computer on board the Apollo 11 lunar module that landed on the moon had the same microprocessor speed as a conventional mobile phone in the year 2000.

The earliest work behind internet technology (transaction of information)

The *Probability* theory and *Queuing* theory were used in the very early days of telephone communications. Queuing theory had directed most of its effort towards single-node facilities with storage. There was a breakthrough when multi-node nets with no storage capabilities were proposed.

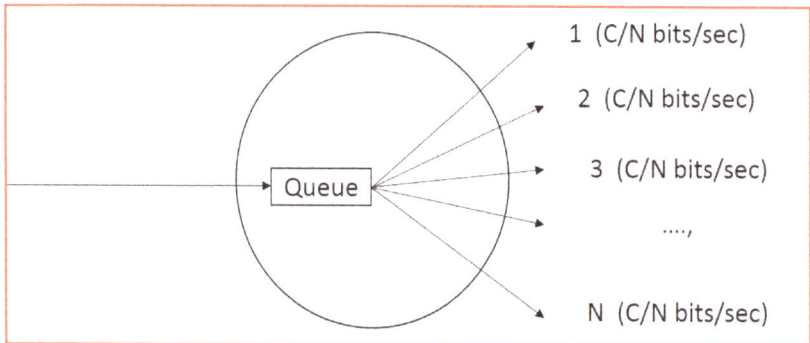

Figure 13: **The initial stages of flow of information in a network**

The above image illustrates the fundamental change in the way information transaction was changed in the 1960s. In the 1970s, the *Advanced Research Projects Agency Network (ARPANET)* implemented the TCP/IP protocol suite. These protocols are a set of rules governing how information is related between computers in a network. New terms like packets, data, webpages, internet service providers (ISPs) arose. The dial-up speed was 0.0024 megabytes per second. The technology had switched from phone line to Digital Subscriber Line (DSL).

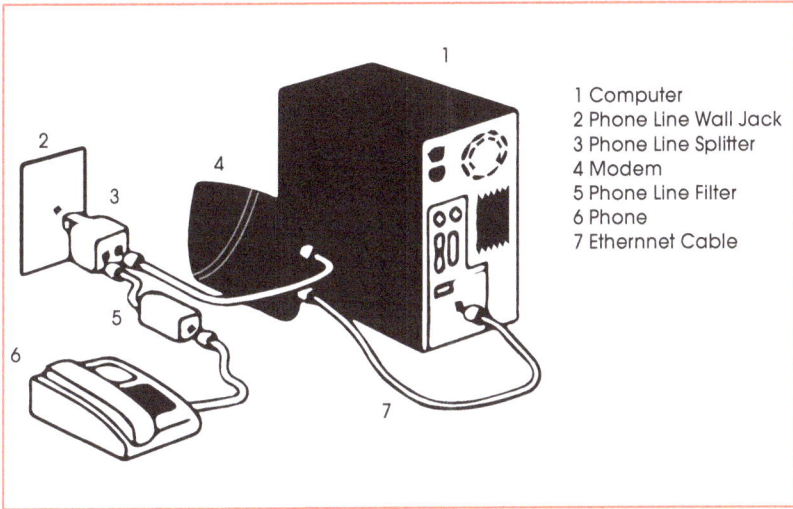

1 Computer
2 Phone Line Wall Jack
3 Phone Line Splitter
4 Modem
5 Phone Line Filter
6 Phone
7 Ethernnet Cable

Figure 14: Digital Subscriber Line (DSL)

DSL sent the data on a different frequency allowing the users to be online and on the phone at the same time. The internet speed has now reached a maximum speed of over 150 megabytes per second. The leap-frog in the technology of transfer of information could be applied to the technology of cash transfer and the underlying blockchain technology.

TCP/IP technology is used in multiple applications in addition to the internet itself: file transfer protocol (for sending larger files), simple mail transfer protocol (SMTP), Telnet protocol, border gateway protocol, internet relay chat and others. Similar blockchain technology could be used for more than cryptocurrency applications.

Asymmetric encryption

Asymmetric encryption is used in many applications like a secure website (https), *Secure Shell*, or Bitcoin. The customers can exchange and share the public keys with others. A private key is required to unlock the document / piece of information and has to be well protected. Bitcoin uses asymmetric encryption to ensure that only the owner of the money wallet can withdraw or transfer money from it.

Browsers are the main portals where all users share their information such as username, password, account details, credit card details, tax file number and so on. RSA (Rivest Shamir Adleir) is an asymmetric encryption algorithm used by computers to encrypt and decrypt messages.

This layer of encryption became more complex as more people started using devices connected to the internet (personal computers, mobile phones, tablets, laptop computers, digital audio players, digital cameras, modern printers...). As of July 2018, Advanced Encryption Standard (AES 128, AES 192, AES 256), Triple Data Encryption Standard (3DES), RSA (Ron Rivest, Adi Shamir and Len Adelman) are some of the most secure encryption methods. (Read further in the following section titled *Secure Hash Algorithm SHA 256*)

If the website has a green padlock on it, then its means that data sent from the browser to the web server and vice-versa are encrypted. The information shared on this website is secured from attackers and hackers. (Watch for the *https padlock* in all the websites where you are sharing your personal and private information)

← → C 🔒 https://www.spacex.com

Connection is secure

Your information (for example, passwords or credit
card numbers) is private when it is sent to this site.
Learn more

Figure 15: **Signs of a secure website with a lock symbol (https
stands for hyper text transfer protocol secured)**

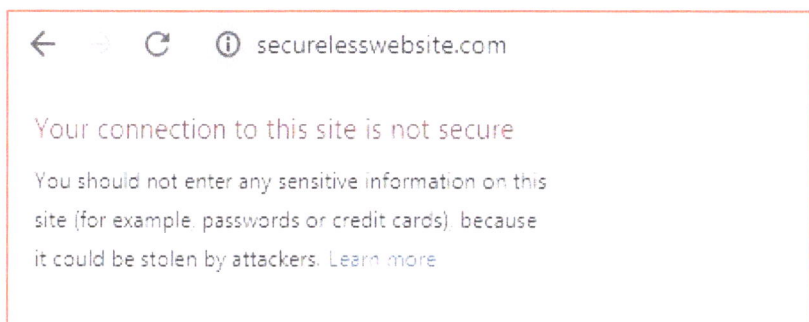

← → C ⓘ securelesswebsite.com

Your connection to this site is not secure

You should not enter any sensitive information on this
site (for example, passwords or credit cards) because
it could be stolen by attackers. Learn more

Figure 16: **Website not secure**

Figure 17: **Signs of a safe and secure website**

Table 4: SSL and DNS acronyms and meanings		
Layer	**Acronym**	**Meaning**
Secure sockets layer	SSL	Webpage is secure
Domain level certificate (Domain Name System)	DNS	Domain level is secure

Internet

The Internet is a global network of computers. Blockchain is a new technology that utilises the global network of computers located in all offices, homes, organisations and universities. Bitcoin and other cryptocurrencies are applications that run on the blockchain technology.

The Internet started small among computers within closed rooms, then eventually expanded to private organisations (intranet) and then servers to the public domain (internet). The internet is not owned by one person.

In 1961, Leonard Kleinrock published a paper titled *Information Flow in Large Communication Nets*. This paper was the basis of flow of information via nets and the article laid the foundation for the technology called the *Internet*. It took over 30 years until Tim Berners-Lee introduced *hypertext mark-up language* (html). This plays a huge part in how we use the internet today. From the first server used by Tim Berners-Lee at CERN (1991), it has reached 100 million servers across the world. The computers in homes are not servers but clients that access the servers. The clients (home computers) are connected to the server via an internet service provider (ISP) like Telstra, Optus or iiNet. This technology has made the World Wide Web (WWW) accessible to the public.

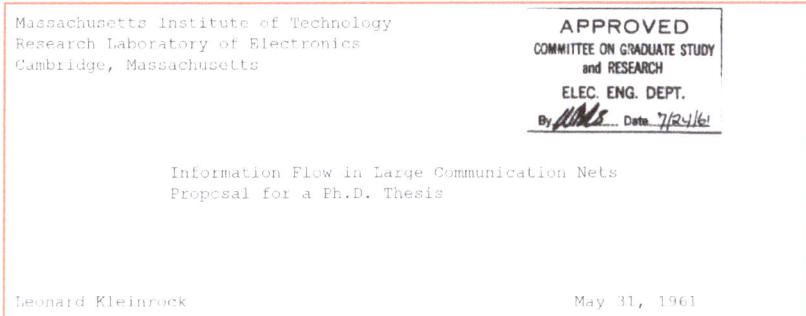

Massachusetts Institute of Technology
Research Laboratory of Electronics
Cambridge, Massachusetts

APPROVED
COMMITTEE ON GRADUATE STUDY
and RESEARCH
ELEC. ENG. DEPT.
By *[signature]* Date 7/24/61

Information Flow in Large Communication Nets
Proposal for a Ph.D. Thesis

Leonard Kleinrock   May 31, 1961

Figure 18: Thesis submitted by Leonard in 1961

An analogy could be drawn between this article published by *Leonard Kleinrock* and the article published by Satoshi. The technology behind the financial technology (credit cards, SWIFT, wire transfer) that was designed before the invention of the internet was a bottleneck in the globalised world where information flows faster – but not the cash, nor currency.

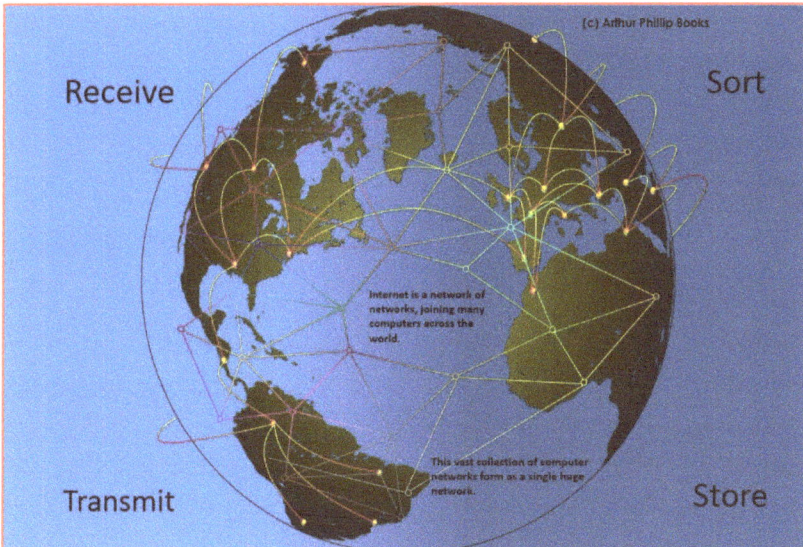

Figure 19: Pictorial representation of various functions of the internet (receive, transmit, store, sort)

Safety on the internet

Encryption

Cyber security is becoming increasingly important as the world becomes more interconnected. In opening channels of communication and information, the internet also poses a greater risk of unauthorised access to your personal data and information. Cybercriminals use technology to take advantage of this; threats are constantly evolving, and increasing in volume and complexity.

Encrypting vs Hashing

Encryption is a process of converting data into a series of unreadable or complex combinations that are not of fixed length. The encrypted string of data can be reverted into its original decrypted form using the correct key. Hashing is an ideal method to store passwords, as hashes are inherently one-way in nature. A password in hash format makes it difficult for someone to reverse the data.

Hashing

Hashing is a process by which any digital file can be converted into a fixed length. This becomes critical when dealing with large numbers, larger file sizes, large amounts of data and transactions.

A hash is a string of random-looking characters that uniquely identifies the data (image, file, password), much like one's finger print. A hash function takes an input that could be a piece of text, or an image or file that always has the same length. A hash function is different from encryption because it only works in one way. An image or text or password can be hashed, but the hash cannot be turned into an image or text or password.

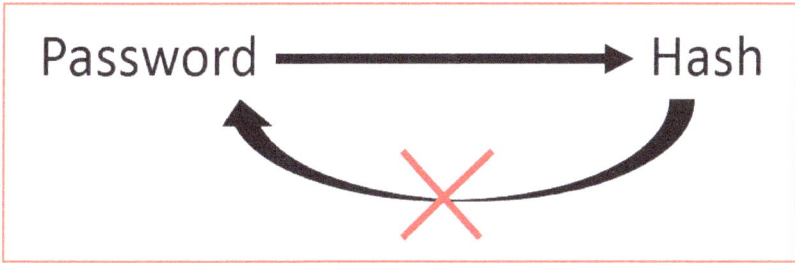

Figure 20: **Unlikely process of reversal of hash to password**

In cryptocurrency, hashing is an important part of the mining process and GPUs are capable of hashing at higher rates than a normal Central Processing Unit (CPU). A battery of computers with multiple CPUs or GPUs is common in a venue where cryptocurrency is being mined and manufacturers of these CPUs and GPUs are aware of the special requirements of miners. There are more products arising in the market that provide high hashing capacity and computing power like a recent one called Application Specific Integrated Circuits (ASIC). Hashing capacity and computing power are the key functions of such machines and they calculate hundreds of thousands of hashes in a second. There are over 25 hashing algorithms. Hash rate is specified as the number of hashes per second. (One kilo is 10^3, one tera is 10^{12}). One terahash is 10^{12} hashes per second = 1 followed by 12 zeros = 1,000,000,000,000 hashes per second). A modern GPU can perform with a speed of 290 million hashes per second.

Secure Hash Algorithm

Secure hash algorithm (SHA) is a cryptographic hash function. Hash function is not cyphering but is a rule that decides the output. In modern computing systems, passwords represent critical information. Hash plays a significant role in securing the system. A good hash function has the following properties:

1. Difficult or impossible to undo
2. A small change in the input produces a major change in the output
3. Number of outputs must be large enough that a table of outputs cannot be constructed or recreated

A cryptographic hash is like a signature for a text or a data file. Hash is a unique one-way function, meaning it cannot be crypted back. There are many types of SHA functions: SHA1, SHA256, SHA384, SHA512, RipeMD128, RipeMD160. The word 'hello' can be hashed into various formats.

String (original file)	hello	Hello
SHA-1	aaf4c61ddcc5e8a2dabede0f3b482cd9aea9434d	f7ff9e8b7bb2e09b70935a5d785e0cc5d9d0abf0
SHA-256	2cf24dba5fb0a30e26e83b2ac5b9e29e1b161e5c1f a7425e73043362938b9824	185f8db32271fe25f561a6fc938b2e264306ec304e da518007d1764826381969
SHA-384	59e1748777448c69de6b800d7a33bbfb9ff1b463e 44354c3553bcdb9c666fa90125a3c79f90397bdf5f 6a13de828684f	3519fe5ad2c596efe3e276a6f351b8fc0b03db8617 82490d45f7598ebd0ab5fd5520ed102f38c4a5ec8 34e98668035fc
SHA-512	9b71d224bd62f3785d96d46ad3ea3d73319bfbc28 90caadae2dff72519673ca72323c3d99ba5c11d7c7 acc6e14b8c5da0c4663475c2e5c3adef46f73bcdec 043	3615f80c9d293ed7402687f94b22d58e529b8cc79 16f8fac7fddf7fbd5af4cf777d3d795a7a00a16bf7e 7f3fb9561ee9baae480da9fe7a18769e71886b03f 315
RipeMD128	789d569f08ed7055e94b4289a4195012	eb507c265df625d5aa16c08f64cd0e65
RipeMD160	108f07b8382412612c048d07d13f814118445acd	d44426aca8ae0a69cdbc4021c64fa5ad68ca32fe

Figure 21: The word "Hello" in various encryptions

Secure Hash Algorithm SHA 256

Cryptocurrency uses SHA algorithm which is a mathematic operation that takes any digital data and outputs a 256 bit number. This was developed by BSA and is widely used in security applications and protocols SSL, PGP, SSH and more so in the internet and other web applications. SHA256 generates an almost unique 256 bit (32 byte) signature for a text at a rate of 1 terahash per second (1 power 12 hash per second).

SHA256 is 256 bits long, equivalent to 32 bytes, or 64 bytes in hexadecimal string format

- 1 byte = 8 bits (8 binary digits)
- 32 bytes = 256 bits

Example: Secure Hash Algorithm 256 is used in Bitcoin. Whatever the size of data block information that SHA256 processes, it always ends up in a 256 bit length. This is very convenient to remember the hash and keep track of transactions by a universally repeatable alphanumeric string.

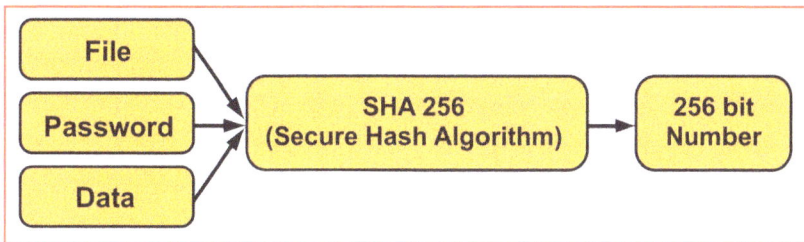

Figure 22: **Steps involved in Secure Hash Algorithm 256**

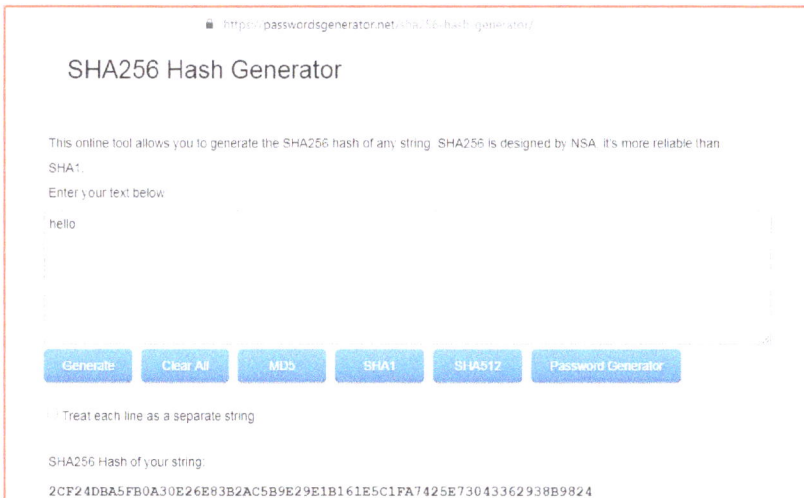

Figure 23: **A screenshot from SHA256 Hash generator for the word 'hello'**

There are many different types of cryptographic hash functions.

- MD5 hash function produces 128 bit hash.
- SHA256 hash function produces 256 bit hash (used in Bitcoin).
- Keccak256 hash function produces 256 bit hash (used in Ethereum).

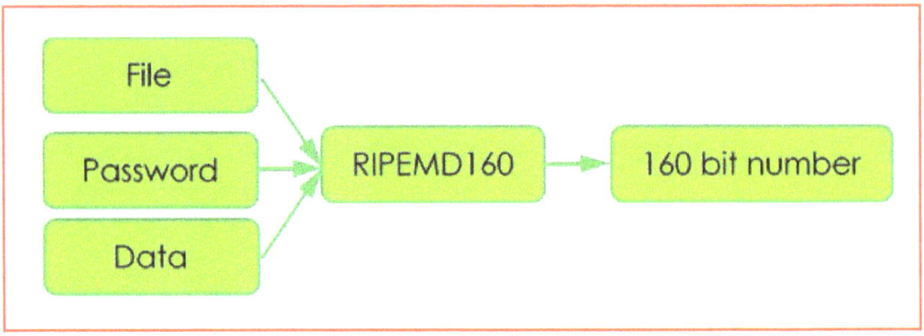

Figure 24: Steps involved in RIPEMD 160

SHA256 to hash a digest that starts with X amounts of 0's. X varies by how much mining power is on the network.

X varies by how much mining power is on the network.

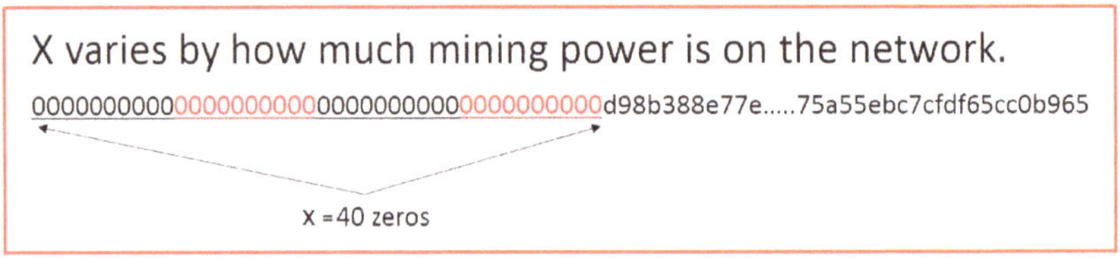

Figure 25: An example of hash with 40 leading zeros

In this above example of 40 leading zeros, it takes over one trillion steps to find a hash where the first 40 bits are equal to zero. There are one trillion steps to compute and it requires a lot of computers and lots of miners. There are over 12,000 mining nodes across the world. This entire network trying to solve a problem could take an average of ten minutes. In 2009, it required a standard desktop computer to do the hashing but in 2017, it requires more power in order to perform the same task.

Each cryptocurrency has its own hash algorithm. With *Bitcoin*, miners are designed to calculate the SHA-256 hash algorithm; for *Litecoin*, it is *Scrypt*.

3   Blockchain – Origin and Purpose

Some people likened blockchain and Bitcoin to the example of the chicken and the egg with some people arguing that, without Bitcoin, blockchain would not exist and others arguing that, without blockchain, Bitcoin would not exist. What we do know is that while Bitcoin and other cryptocurrencies take the limelight, blockchain – the technology – works tirelessly in the background. As blockchain is starting to be incorporated into various technologies, there is a misconception that blockchain is Bitcoin. This is certainly not the case.

What we do know is that, in early 2009, a person working under the pseudonym of Satoshi Nakamoto released a working beta version of the Bitcoin and blockchain technology. The mystery of who Satoshi Nakamoto really is may remain unsolved as he, or she, disappeared from the scene in 2010. Since that time, many people, including an Australian by the name of Craig Wright, have claimed to be Satoshi Nakamoto.

We are on the brink of another technology revolution and an application as part of the revolution: blockchain is the technology and cryptocurrency is the currency application. But blockchain has much more to offer than just being considered a ledger for financial transactions as we will see over the next few chapters.

Blockchain could be compared to the internet. From a very small market share in the 1990s, the internet has grown exponentially and now enjoys a huge market share worth around seven trillion dollars.

This huge market creates a constant demand for new technology and makes the world smaller and more connected. The global economy has been changing rapidly.

Every day thousands of container ships enter hundreds of ports and millions of passengers board thousands of aircraft around the world; every corner of the earth is now linked to every other more than ever before. Free trade agreements and open markets bind nations together.

The financial markets between countries are more connected and the daily currency exchange between countries is worth around 6.5 trillion dollars. Our businesses are global but our currencies are national. The middle men in all the associated businesses are many and hence the chances of errors as well as malpractices are high. All stakeholders want to minimise the risks and maximise the returns.

What is blockchain?

Blockchain is a developing technology and represents a type of 'next generation business process improvement' software that was unthinkable a few decades ago. It is, however, based on the simple idea of a ledger which maintains the entire history of transactions. Ledgers have been around for centuries and are basically a book for recording regular transactions; for example, in accounting, monies owed and paid. Computer software like MYOB and Quicken does this in the background once information is input.

Let's look at some of the defining features of the blockchain technology:

Blockchain is the engine behind all cryptocurrencies and ensures that transactions between two individuals cannot be undone by others and the same coin is not spent twice by multiple people. This ensures that coins are not duplicated illegally. This is achieved primarily by using the concept of 'safety in numbers'; one person could change one copy of a ledger but they cannot change millions of copies of ledgers at the same time. If one person could change their local copy, the rest of the network would reject such updates as they are constantly, and publicly, verifying the correct version of the ledger. Blockchain is storing a block of transactions appropriately encoded across multiple computers spread around the world and cross-verifying them almost continuously. This continuous cross-referencing and verification makes it almost impossible to corrupt or modify the information related to transactions.

Terminology and how it works

In order to understand blockchain a little better, we can simplify blockchain into individual parts – the block and the chain. Each block contains transactions or a collection of data. For example, in sending Bitcoin from party A to party B, the details of that transaction, including its source, destination and date/time stamp, are added to the block. When a transaction is made and information is added to a block, that information cannot be edited or removed thereby ensuring the reliability and security of the blockchain. This highlights another of blockchain's benefits: its transparency. When the block contains all the information required, it is then added to the one that came before it and then the next block is added to this block to form the chain. A signature is generated for each block, which is then added to the next block, thus 'chaining' them together. In this way, any changes to a previous block will change its signature, which changes the next block, and so on. This is how the blockchain protects the ledger from being changed or tampered.

If you can imagine a goods train, each block is a wagon which, when loaded and verified, is added to the train.

Most blockchains are simple unbroken chains but there are others that assemble blocks in a web-like structure or that run chains off the side of the main blockchain.

Similar to the internet, the blockchain network is global. The application, or the technology, can be banned but it cannot be shut down unless all the computers on the network are switched off physically.

Components of a blockchain

Blockchain is a distributed ledger that is publicly available to anyone who has access to the internet. Once data has been recorded inside a blockchain, it becomes very difficult to change it. The data that is stored inside a block depends on the type of blockchain.

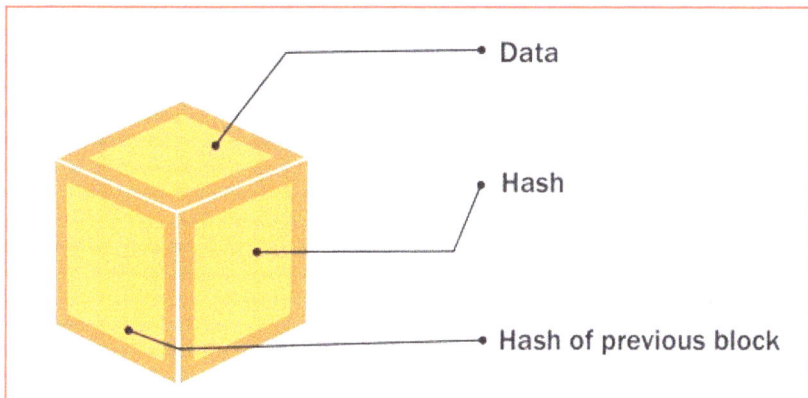

Figure 26: **Generic components of a block (data, hash and hash of previous block)**

A Bitcoin blockchain would have details such as information about the sender, receiver and the amount of coins. Bitcoin is a digital currency that is implemented with software (Bitcoin protocol). The protocol establishes the rule that everyone should agree to if they want to use Bitcoin. The protocol details how large a block is, how fees are calculated, and how much the miners receive.

This block also has a hash similar to a fingerprint. It identifies a block and all of its contents, and is always unique, just as a fingerprint. Once the block is created, its hash is being calculated. If someone tries to tamper with the block by changing the hash inside the block, it will cause the hash to change. The hash is very useful when one wants to detect changes to blocks.

Figure 27: Schematics of Bitcoin blockchain (data, hash and hash of previous block)

Genesis block

The first block in the chain is the genesis block. The sequence of all blocks and its interconnectivity makes it tamper-proof. Changing a single block will make all subsequent blocks invalid.

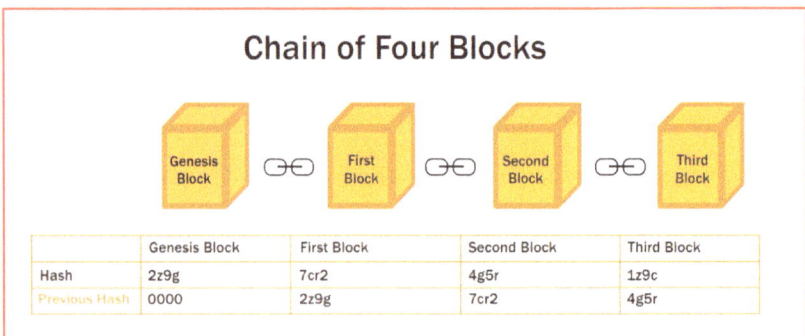

Chain of Four Blocks

	Genesis Block	First Block	Second Block	Third Block
Hash	2z9g	7cr2	4g5r	1z9c
Previous Hash	0000	2z9g	7cr2	4g5r

Figure 28: Schematics of chain of four blocks including genesis block

Proof-of-work

Proof-of-work is a technique that sustains the creation of new blocks in a blockchain. In Bitcoin's blockchain, proof-of-work takes about 10 minutes to calculate and add a new block to the chain. The mechanism makes it harder to tamper with a block in a chain. If one block was tampered with, then the person involved in tampering would have to recalculate the proof-of-work for all the following blocks. There is a fundamental overlaying structure on which blockchain is constructed: it is being distributed. Blockchain is a peer-to-peer network and everyone who has access to the internet is allowed to join. When someone joins such a network, the person has access to the full copy of the blockchain.

Creation of a new block in the system

Another defining feature of the blockchain technology is that of cryptography which is simply a process that requires a mathematical equation to be solved before transactions are recorded on the blockchain. Cryptography is not new and is also involved in regular bank transactions. Cryptography is a way of mapping a sequence of numbers or letters into another sequence such that the reverse mapping is nearly impossible to perform unless one knows how the first mapping was performed.

The process of generating the signature for a block involves a hash function. Hash functions are not new and are a way of mapping a sequence of numbers or letters into a fixed length series of numbers and letters such that the reverse mapping is nearly impossible to perform without having the original input.

This ensures that the only people involved in the first mapping can perform the reverse mapping to get the original sequence. When a transaction occurs between two individuals, that transaction cannot be undone by any other person other than the original pair when the transaction is cryptographically encoded. (We have included a section on cryptography in *Chapter one* in this book).

There are two types of blockchain: public and private. Those who are allowed to participate in the network, execute the consensus protocol and maintain the shared ledger, is the sole distinction between public and private blockchains.

As the name suggests, a public blockchain is completely open allowing anyone to join and participate in the network. For example, with Bitcoin being a public blockchain, there is little or no privacy for transactions and they require substantial computational power to maintain a distributed ledger on a large scale.

A private blockchain network is normally a permissible network based on a business. There are only a few methods of entry for participation in the network such as existing participants allowing a future entrant, a consortium making the decision, or a regulatory authority issuing a licence to allow participation. Each entrant that joins a private blockchain has a role in maintaining the blockchain in a decentralised manner. Private blockchains offer lower cost and faster speed than public blockchains.

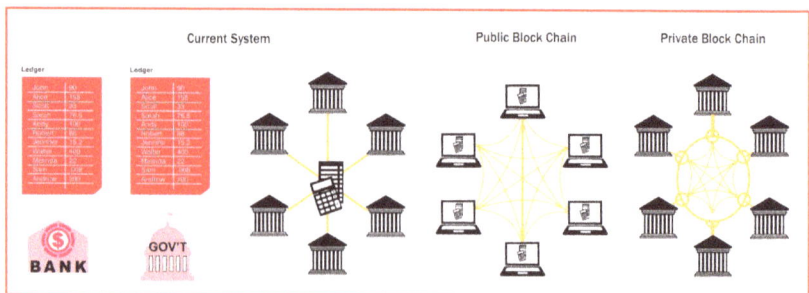

Figure 29: **Public blockchain and private blockchain**

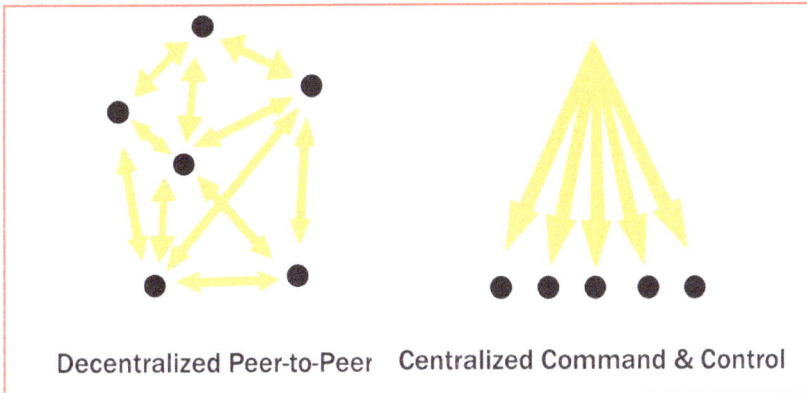

Decentralized Peer-to-Peer   Centralized Command & Control

Figure 30: Arrow diagram illustrating decentralised and centralised systems

Early in the history of money, the people who were entrusted with gold, and who issued certificates of holding to the owners of gold, eventually became greedy and distributed more certificates of holding than the gold they had in reserve. The resulting inflation, and the distrust leading to a run on these 'banks', is a classic example of a central authority's misdeeds leading to real economic crashes.

Before the invention of the printing press, knowledge was centralised in certain individuals and organisations such as the nobles and the church. The printing press revolutionised the availability of knowledge in the form of books, pamphlets and so on. In the past 400 years, education, printing and sharing knowledge has become cheaper and more accessible to the public.

A centralized authority that performs transaction verification and secures money against duplication can grow into a powerful institution with leverage over the supply of money itself, as has happened in the past century across the world. A healthy mistrust in the central authority is needed for all forms of society to keep the interests of the many intact against the greed of the few. Blockchain is created with the explicit purpose of undercutting the authority of centralized control over the flow of money.

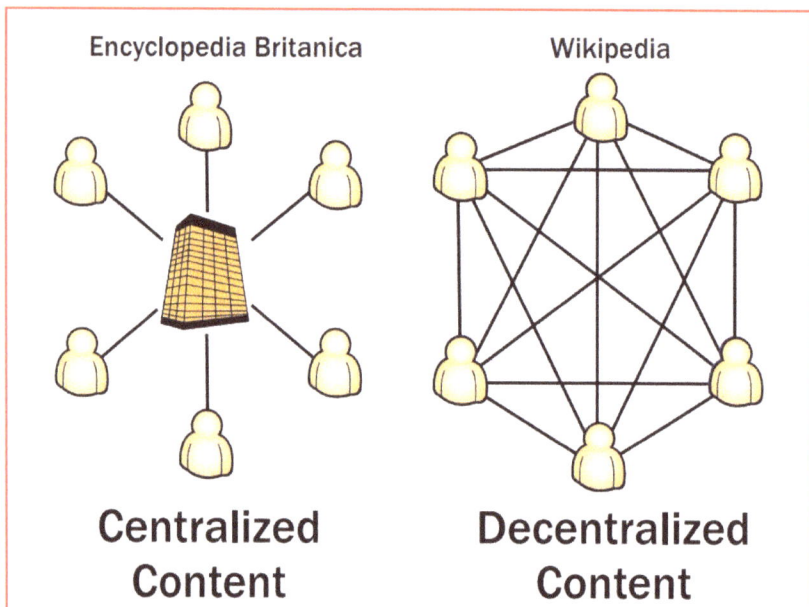

Encyclopedia Britanica

Wikipedia

Centralized Content

Decentralized Content

Figure 31: Illustration comparing Encyclopaedia Britannica and Wikipedia

In the above example of Encyclopaedia Britannica (centralised content) and Wikipedia (decentralised content), they both serve the same purpose (and are also indistinguishable) except that the Britannica can be viewed and be read with no currency of information. The decentralised content of Wikipedia is live and refreshed every few seconds. The decentralised application like blockchain would serve the same purpose as its centralised counterpart.

Amenities and organisations like radio stations, power plants, railroad networks, newspaper printing services, and large manufacturers are centralised for easier distribution and to minimise the cost involved in operations. Some of the aforementioned concepts have moved to decentralisation; for example, power generation via solar panels on houses have undermined the concepts of decentralisation. The internet is another classic example. However, when a concept or authority becomes centralised or monopolised, it often dampens innovation and transparency in the system. These concepts of authority (centralisation) sometimes threaten the fabric of society. When the power plant shuts down or the radio station malfunctions, the transmission of power and radio to their patrons is completely cut off. These centralisation concepts in the current era may need to be redesigned or re-engineered for the internet age, where data and information are integral.

In the world of capitalism, every thing is identified by certain parameters (name, number, identification, photo proof, tax file number, social security number, driving licence number, and much more). In the computer world, these are converted into a sequence of numbers and letters. There is more trust in a system that is more secure.

Trust is a key component in our social lives. Humans need trust to coordinate and to cooperate with one another.

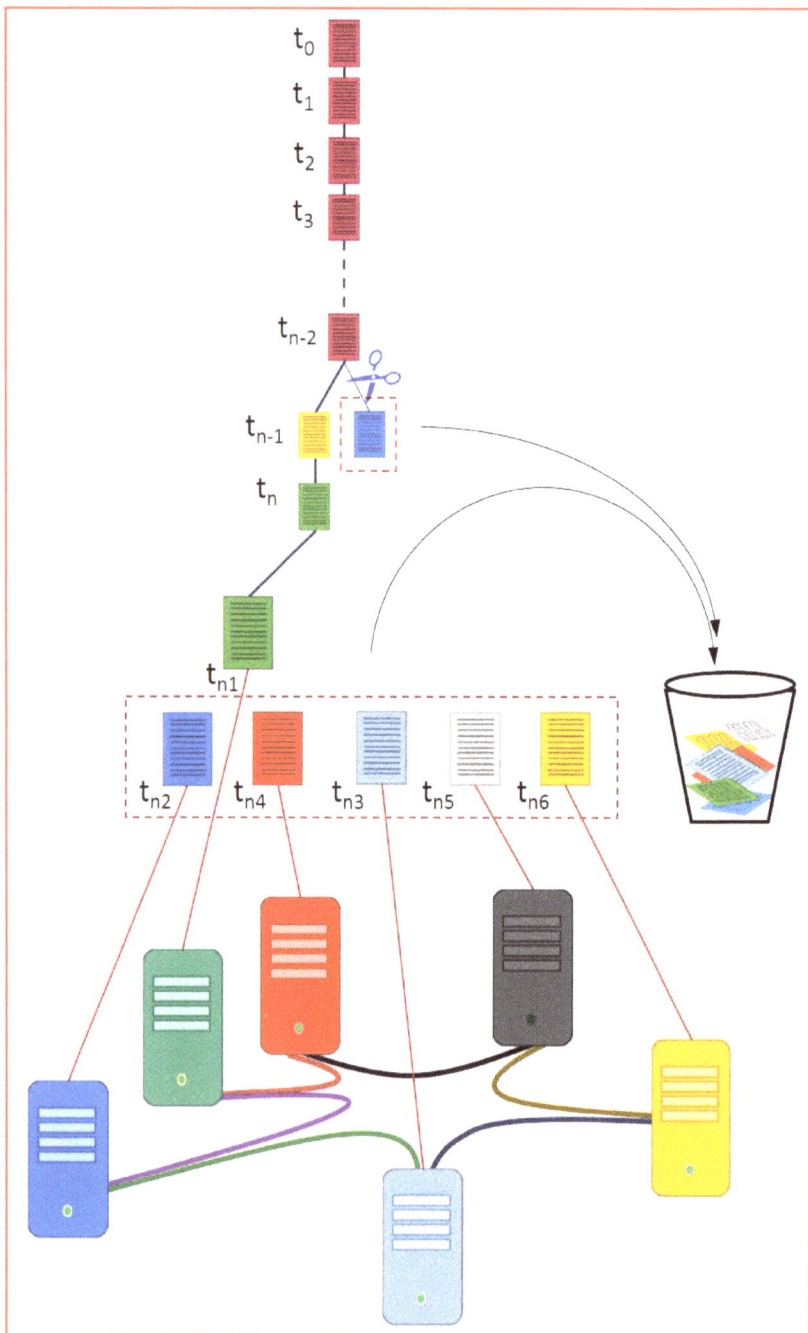

Figure 32: Sequence of steps involved in the validation of a transaction in a blockchain protocol

Blockchain aims to remove the middleman concept and make it more efficient in many industries. Blockchain is a new way of managing trust among stakeholders.

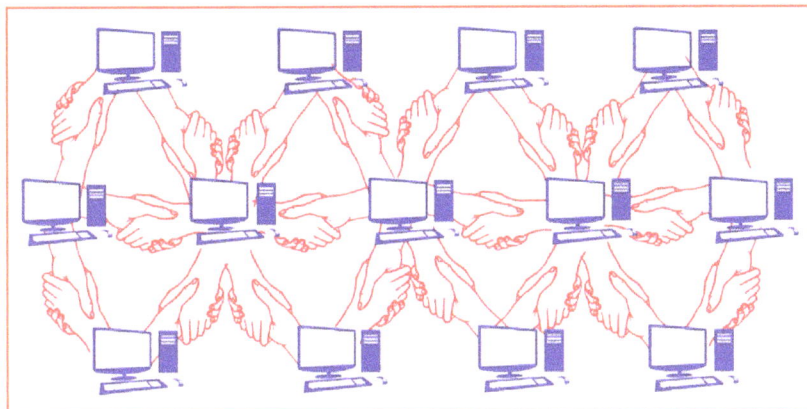

Figure 33: Blockchain (handshake protocol) among all the computers in the network

Global business is based on a new way of managing trust. The basic protocol is the success of any technology. The internet has a workable protocol called TCP/IP. This protocol is the baseline protocol, on which toolset layer and application are built.

Table 5: Difference between internet technology and blockchain technology		
	Internet	Blockchain
Base layer protocol or formula or recipe	TCP/IP	Blockchain protocol
Toolset layer (second layer)	http	Still in progress
Application layer (third or top layer)	Email, online bank accounts	Still in progress

Mistakes often occur in the second and third layer where the email is hacked or bank accounts are compromised. The base layer protocol is strong and hence the internet is able to cope with huge volume transactions including a total capacity of one billion webpages. If the email is hacked, it means that a mistake happened at application level or user level. The email protocol is strong but not suitable for a next generation of global business. There is a demand for an internet upgrade. Blockchain could be one of the alternatives.

Blockchain has a unique feature in a time stamp and a smart contract embedded in various applications. These smart features were not available in any software in the past. This means that the trail cannot be tampered with at all and makes all processes more transparent. There are many instances in the past where an individual or an organisation has made mistakes and has erased trails to avoid any potential damage to themselves or to the organisations.

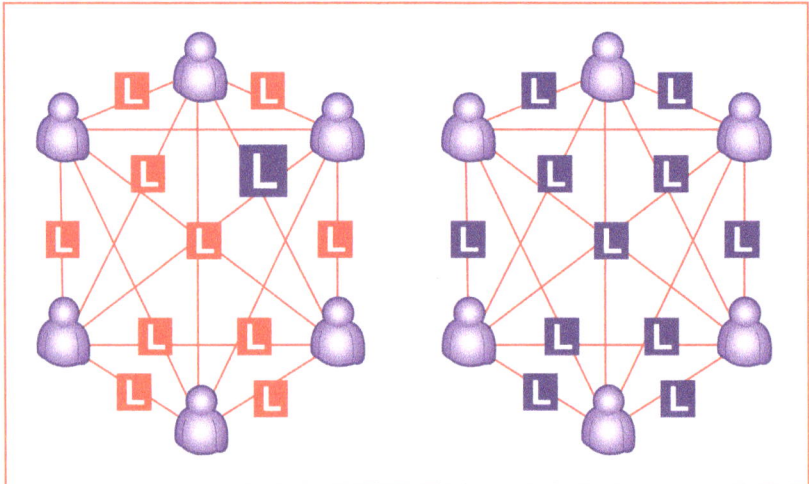

Figure 34: **The process of achieving consensus in a blockchain system**

Forking

Similar to the natural evolution of a product, forking of various applications is plausible; however, the chances of survival of the best application are higher.

Bitcoin is the mother of all cryptocurrencies. There have been over 1600 cryptocurrencies created since 2009. Cryptocurrencies are becoming more and more popular. There are more developers coming with their own ideology to improvise the underlying protocol and fork into different products. There are two types of forking: hard forking and soft forking. Hard fork happens when some developer forks Bitcoin and makes it incompatible with the original. Soft fork happens when the developer forks Bitcoin and makes it compatible with Bitcoin.

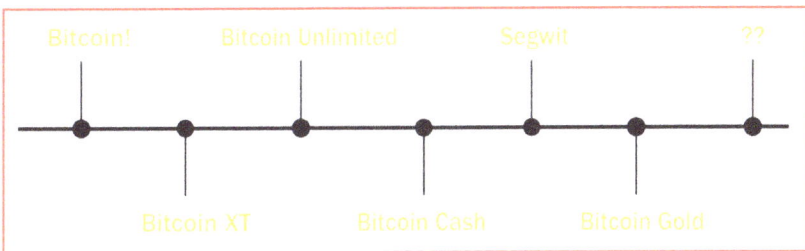

Figure 35: **The process of forking in cryptocurrencies**

Some users and developers might disagree with the direction that Bitcoin is taking. Bitcoin consists of two major pieces of information: Bitcoin protocol and blockchain. Bitcoin is an open source code, hence addition / amendment to the protocol is feasible.

On 1st August 2017, *Bitcoin Cash* was born as part of hard forking. The developers could not agree on what the size of a block should be (1 MB, 2 MB, or over). Over a few short years, Bitcoin has had a number of forks already like *Bitcoin XT, Bitcoin Unlimited, Bitcoin Cash, Segwit,* and *Bitcoin Gold.*

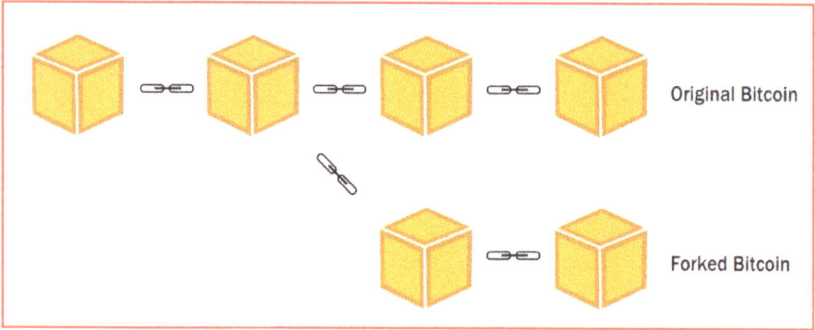

Figure 36: **Original bitcoin vs forked bitcoin**

4   Current Uses of Blockchain

While there are some companies in Australia either using or trialling blockchain, there are many more worldwide. Some of the terminology here may be less familiar to Australians.

Automotive industries

Regular odometers can be replaced with smart odometers that are connected to the internet and frequently update the car's odometer reading onto the blockchain. This would create a secure and digital certificate for each automobile. *Bosch Internet of Things* labs are currently testing this model in Europe.

Banking

In 2017, ANZ and Westpac Banks used blockchain for bank guarantees on commercial property leasing.

An Israeli bank and Microsoft are collaborating on a blockchain for managing bank guarantees.

Barclays are looking at a number of blockchain initiatives primarily involving compliance and combating fraud as well as tracking financial transactions.

ABRA is a cryptocurrency wallet utilising the Bitcoin blockchain to hold and track balances stored in different currencies.

Charities

Working with charities such as *Save the Children, The Water Project and Medic Mobile, Bitgive* aims to provide greater transparency to charity donations by providing clearer links between giving and the project outcomes.

Cybersecurity

In Estonia, *Guardtime* is creating a 'keyless' signature system used to secure that country's health records.

A decentralised authentication system being developed by REMME aims to replace logins and passwords with SSL certificates stored on a blockchain.

Financial Services

The Australian Stock Exchange (ASX) is trialling blockchain to replace its *Clearing House Electronic Subregister System* (CHESS) equities clearing and settlement system, with a proposed implementation in early 2018. The ASX has been trialling a distributed ledger technology for over two and a half years.

The University of Sydney has been developing the *Red Belly* blockchain to process financial transactions with latest test results showing more than 660,000 transactions per second being achieved. (Note: The Visa network peak capacity is around 56,000 transactions per second).

Aeternity allows for automated payments of smart contracts to be made when parties agree that conditions have been met.

Augur allows for the trading of derivatives and other financial instruments in a decentralised ecosystem.

Food industry

The food industry can implement blockchain technology from the harvest to when produce ends up in the hands of consumers. Blockchain could help the food industry to create a digital certificate for each piece of food, showing –

- where it originated
- how it was transported
- what batch it belongs to
- who has been in contact with it

Walmart in the USA and *IBM* are working on technology to make the tracing of food products quicker and more transparent.

Freight

Maersk, the world's largest shipping company is looking to blockchain to manage its cargo. In the tests, Dutch customs and *US Homeland Security* were able to remotely access data about the cargo.

UPS, an international shipping company, is currently looking at using blockchain in its customs brokerage business and has joined the *Blockchain in Trucking Alliance* which is working to develop blockchain standards for the freight industry.

FedEx, another shipping giant has also joined the Blockchain in Trucking Alliance and has launched a pilot program of blockchain to help solve customer disputes. FedEx also hopes to use blockchain to store records.

Government

In March 2018, Sierra Leone became the first country to use the blockchain technology in its elections. The blockchain solution was developed by *Agora*, a Switzerland-based voting technology company. In association with the European Commission, the *Red Cross* and the *Swiss Federal Institute of Technology, University of Fribourg*, the blockchain distributed ledger tracked the election which was contested by 16 candidates.

A few weeks later, Sierra Leone's National Electoral Commission denied that blockchain was used in the elections.

Followmyvote.com is another that aims to create a secure, transparent voting system, reducing opportunities for voter fraud and increasing turnout through improved accessibility.

In partnership with *Ericsson*, the Estonian government is looking to place public records onto the blockchain.

Public safety and transport applications are targeted to be put onto blockchain in a joint venture between the South Korean Government and *Samsung*.

The Department of Works and Pensions in the United Kingdom is investigating blockchain to record and administer benefit payments.

In 2016, a committee representing 30 government departments of the United Arab Emirates was formed to investigate opportunities across health records, shipping, business registration, and to prevent the spread of conflict diamonds.

Healthcare

Smart contracts can be used to store medical records on a blockchain and doctors would only be allowed to access them when approved with a digital signature. The patron could store personal identity details on the smart contract and choose what data to reveal.

Massachusetts Institute of Technology (MIT) MedRec project is designed to manage authentication, confidentiality and data sharing of medical records.

SimplyVital Health is also looking at patient records and their project, *ConnectingCare*, is designed to track the progress of patients after they leave hospital.

A startup called *GEM* is working with the Centre for Disease Control to record disease outbreak data on blockchain in order to increase disaster relief and response effectiveness.

Insurance

Maersk, is hoping to use blockchain to streamline marine insurance. Smart contracts in blockchains can be used by insurance companies to validate claims and calculate payouts.

Smart contracts could also be used for car insurance so that customers only pay for insurance for the time they are driving.

Intellectual Property

The online website *stampd.io* allows users to add documents to the Bitcoin or *Ethereum* blockchain. Once the data is added onto the blockchain, the data is time stamped and notarized. However the blockchain stamping is not on the same level as notaries in a legal perspective.

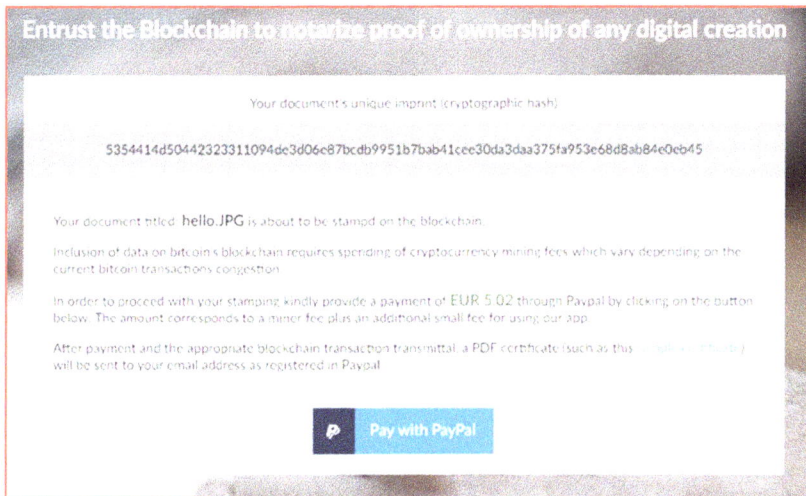

Figure 37: **Electronic notarising using blockchain technology**

Manufacturing

Blockverify is a blockchain platform which has focused on anti-counterfeit measures initially in the diamond, luxury goods and pharmaceutical markets.

Hijro aims to create a blockchain for collaborating on prototyping and proof of concept. It has changed its name from *Fluent*. *Provenance* is another project aimed at providing a blockchain-based provenance record of transparency within the supply chain.

SKUChain is another system being developed to track goods as they go through the supply chain.

STORJ.io is a distributed and encrypted cloud storage system which allows users to share unused hard drive space.

Transactivgrid aims to reduce the costs involved in energy distribution by allowing its members based in Brooklyn to locally produce and sell energy locally.

Media

Kodak, synonymous with photography, is developing a blockchain application to track intellectual property rights and payments to photographers.

Ujomusic aims to record and track royalties for musicians as well as create a record of ownership of their works. Smart contracts can be used in the music industry where the streaming services could collect a fee for the tracks that were accessed by users. The smart contract can also distribute royalties to artists based on how many times their songs have been accessed.

Retail

In the retail arena, *Walmart* is using blockchain to track products from the source to the store and hopes that it may streamline the restocking process.

Blockpoint.io allows retailers to build payment systems around cryptocurrencies, blockchain-derived gift cards and loyalty schemes.

Loyyal aims to allow consumers to combine and trade loyalty rewards in new ways and to allow retailers to offer more sophisticated loyalty packages.

OpenBazaar aims to build a decentralised market where goods and services are traded without a middleman.

Science

The *CSIRO*, Australia's peak science body, has been investigating how to gain productivity benefits through the blockchain technology.

Tourism

The online travel portal, *Webjet,* is developing a blockchain application to allow empty hotel rooms to be tracked and traded efficiently.

Transport

British Airways is reported to be testing blockchain to manage data about flights with the aim of reducing conflicting flight information at gate monitors, airline websites and flight apps.

Arcade City is developing a blockchain for ride-sharing and car hiring.

Similarly, at a community level, *LaZooz* aims for synchronizing empty seats with passengers needing a lift in real-time.

IBM Blockchain Solutions is looking at efficiencies to be gained in the vehicle leasing industry.

Voting

Voting on paper is costly and electronic voting has security issues on a par with tampering of voting papers. Blockchain technology can be used to cast and store votes. Such a system would be very transparent as everyone could verify the vote count and it would make tampering very difficult. *Agora* is a globally-focused technology company that enables verifiable and transparent elections through a revolutionary blockchain e-voting system. The voting system allows anyone, anywhere to vote online from a digital device in a fully secure, simple and assured way.

Australia

In Australia, there are a number of companies pioneering blockchain use. RMIT University has recently announced an eight-week short course in blockchain.

Australia is leading the development of international standards on blockchain development. *Standards Australia* was appointed manager of the secretariat of international organisation for Standardisation *ISO/TC 307 Blockchain and electronic distributed ledger technologies*. Australia has also hosted the first international blockchain standards meeting. Standards Australia is advocating for clear guidelines for developing blockchain applications as well as relevant privacy and security measures. Another key focus is interoperability standards so that blockchains can interact with each other.

Around the world, major companies are experimenting with blockchain, particularly in banking and supply chains.

In October 2017, *Oracle* announced the formation of *Oracle Blockchain Cloud Service* and, in November 2017, Microsoft announced an expansion of its R3 consortium to make it easier for financial institutions to use blockchain in Microsoft's *Azure* cloud.

This is just a small number of companies worldwide that are looking at how blockchain will revolutionise their operations.

5 Future Possibilities of Blockchain and its Rivals

Provision of the distribution of cryptocurrencies like Bitcoin is likely to be a very small part of blockchain's future uses. Because the underlying technology of blockchain can be leveraged in virtually any field, the possibilities for blockchain are almost endless.

Tasks that blockchain is ideally suited to include executing contracts, buying and selling intellectual property, storing and distributing medical information and voting in elections to ensure they are incorruptible.

Blockchain will benefit a wide range of industries, not only financial industries. It is still in its nascent stage and will take some time to make a more positive impact over a wide range of industries.

An analogy could be drawn to the internet in the early 1990s. The early stages of internet infrastructure was so poor that it took a few steps to activate the internet on a computer:

1. Plug the cable from the computer into the modem
2. Switch on the modem
3. Phone up the main computer
4. Wait for the computer to answer

Unfortunately, the internet line would get disconnected when there was an incoming call. The internet technology has exponentially grown mainly due to the initial investment from venture capitalists and then followed by industries and other organisations that directly benefitted from the internet. By 2018, the internet had been adopted by almost all industries from banks to media to transport.

- *Uber* is the largest taxi company but owns no car in its fleet
- *Facebook* has the largest media content but owns no media nor content

- *Alibaba* is the largest retailer with no inventory
- *Airbnb* is the largest accommodation provider with no rooms.

Similarly it can be vaguely inferred that cryptocurrencies are a growing bank with no branches nor employees. As we have previously stated, not all cryptocurrencies are successful and this has been the case in other industries where similar startups to Uber, Facebook, Alibaba and Airbnb arose but did not survive in time.

Smart contract

The term 'smart contract' was first used by *Nick Szabo* in 1997 before the concept of Bitcoin and blockchain arose in 2009. Smart contracts are similar to contracts in paper form. They have one special feature: they are completely digital. They are simple programs that are stored on the blockchain and used to automatically exchange coins based on specific conditions mentioned in the contract. Smart contracts are also used for storing medical records, creating a digital notary or even collecting taxes in the future.

They inherit some special features. Smart contracts are immutable (cannot be tampered with) and they are distributed (consensus in the network). Thus banks can issue loans and payments to its customers, insurance companies can process claims, and post and courier services can get paid on delivery of an item. *Ethereum* is one of the major blockchains that supports smart contracts.

Blockchain and allied applications like smart contracts can be used to verify many types of data. Potential new uses for blockchain are being discovered regularly.

There are many challenges and opportunities behind all these blockchain based applications. There is a lot of work required; in particular creation of architecture or frameworks, or a suitable system to integrate these functionalities into various industries. It is expected that public, open-sourced blockchain will affect the following industries to start with:

Table 6: Various applications of blockchain technology	
Industries	**Impact**
Banking and payment	Blockchain services will provide financial services to billions of people around the world including people in developing countries. The user can transact with others directly without having a central organisation nor financial institution.
Cybersecurity	Blockchain is public but the data is verified and secured by cryptography. Hence the data is secure and resistant to unauthorised changes and hacks
Supply chain management	All transactions are documented in a permanent decentralised record. The transactions are monitored securely and transparently. This can reduce time delay. Blockchain also verifies authenticity or fair trade status of products.
Networking and the Internet of Things (IoT)	Eliminates the need for a central location to handle communications for IoT devices. IoT devices could communicate directly, update software, manage bugs and monitor energy usage.
Forecasting	Research consulting, analysing and forecasting – peer to peer network and crowd-sourcing of data
Insurance	Insured person identities, adding smart contracts, insurance that relies on real world data
Transport and ridesharing	Decentralised concept of peer-to-peer ride-sharing apps. There is no need for a third party to manage the software; the smart contract can manage. Car owners to pay for parking, tolls and fuel automatically.
Cloud storage	Blockchain removes the centralised servers concept. (Centralised servers can be easily hacked that could create data loss). Blockchain allows cloud storage to be more robust and secure against such attacks.
Donations	Removes corruption and makes each step of money handling more transparent. Blockchain technology can track every dollar that has been spent.
Voting	All voting records are publicly viewable. This would make the elections fairer and more democratic. Rigging of electronic voting machines is not possible. It increases security, efficiency and transparency of governmental operations. Other positive attributes include preventing people from voting twice and identification of a citizen before voting.

Table 6: Various applications of blockchain technology	
Industries	**Impact**
Public benefits	Blockchain will help, verify and distribute benefits securely. This could possibly lead to the concept of universal basic income.
Healthcare	Blockchain can assist hospitals and medical facilities to safely keep track of medicines and medical equipment.
Manufacturing	Supply chain management is more robust. Each and every supplier can be tracked. Requirements for vendor qualifications could be eased.
Energy management	Blockchain-based applications could allow customers to buy and sell energy from each other in a decentralised way.
Music industry	Musicians can be paid directly by the customers and patrons that download the music. This may remove the middleman. Smart contracts can also solve licensing and copyright issues. The contracts can also catalogue songs with their respective creators.
Retail	Buyers and sellers connect without a middleman or a company like Alibaba or Amazon. Trust comes in the form of a smart contract system.
Real estate	When buying and selling properties, title insurance could be removed completely as the sequence of title owners could be added onto a smart contract. Mistakes in public records and fraudulent documents could be minimised. It could help track, verify ownership and ensure accuracy of documents and property transfers.
Crowdfunding	Crowdfunding platforms create the bridge between investors and project owners. These platforms also charge a fee. Trust is created through smart contracts and online reputation systems.
Governments	Transparency in the issue of passports, birth/ wedding/death certificates, drivers' licences and social security identification.

Rivals to blockchain

Like the various offshoots that have spawned from the original Bitcoin, there has been a new distributed ledger technology rival to blockchain. The biggest threat to blockchain appears to be *Hashgraph* and newcomers *IOTA* and *Holochain*.

Hashgraph was created by a company called *Swirlds*. Swirlds holds a patent for the hashgraph algorithm and has chosen not to make the code open source. The lack of open source code and lack of a token or a public ledger was a concern to many but a hashgraph token is now available.

In distributed ledger technology, it is essential to reach consensus and in Bitcoin and other blockchain projects, a consensus protocol is used by proof-of-work or proof-of-stake. A number of problems have been identified with these two algorithms namely:

- that it takes a longer time to work,
- the environmental cost (associated with the huge computing power required and power consumption)
- transaction fees, and
- there is difficulty to scale using blockchain. Scalability appears to be one, if not the biggest, drawback of blockchain. Every node has to process every transaction for blockchain to be truly decentralised but the more nodes that are added, the less efficient blockchain becomes.

Some other issues associated with blockchain include wastage of time and resources associated with a stale block. There have also been accusations of bias and unfairness in that the order of transactions is not guaranteed in either the proof-of-work or the proof-of-stake protocols; instead the miners determine the order based on the value of the transaction. This, then, raises the issue of synchronicity where users may have to wait for their transactions to be added to the network.

Dr Leemon Baird invented a virtual voting consensus algorithm and this is used by hashgraph instead of proof-of-work. Hashgraph also uses a gossip protocol which allows nodes in the community to rapidly and efficiently exchange data with other community nodes. This automatically builds a cryptographically secure hashgraph data structure which contains the history of communication in a community. Within the community, nodes run the virtual voting consensus algorithm to reach consensus and timestamp without any further communication.

The hashgraph algorithm needs no proof-of-work or leader system so it can deliver low cost and high performance levels. By using consensus time stamping and preventing any individual from changing the consensus order of transaction, it is a fairer system.

The proof of work method used by blockchain has proven to be incapable of efficiently processing large volumes of transactions.

Ethereum and EOS, known principally as cryptocurrencies, have developed their own respective solutions (still based on the blockchain technology) to the scalability problem but neither have been proven on a large commercial scale.

Another cryptocurrency, IOTA is also developing an innovative spin on the blockchain technology. It is called 'the tangle' and is designed to manage transactions in the so-called *Internet of Things*. The developers of IOTA are aiming to provide a secure way for people to earn money by allowing others access to the unused power in other computers connected to the internet. Unlike bitcoin's peer-to-peer transactions, IOTA is designed on a machine-to-machine level. IOTA, the cryptocurrency, was designed as a universal method of payment.

The Tangle is a decentralised peer-to-peer or machine-to-machine network which does not rely on block mining or an external consensus process. Instead, it allows secure data transfers directly between digital devices in a self-regulated manner and without transaction fees. Different devices use different protocols to interact with the network so one of IOTA's goals is to streamline this process. *Snapshotting* is used to handle data on the Tangle ledger to efficiently process many transaction at once and therefore address the problem of scaling. IOTA is also working to create clients in several different programming languages so that the system is flexible for developers.

A more radical approach has been taken by *Holochain* which, technically, is not using blockchain technology. The Holochain ICO occurred in April 2018, so it is a very new technology. Holochain has no consensus or single ledger, nor even a global shared state. With blockchain, data is downloaded from a single source – the ledger of all transactions comprising the blockchain. In contrast, Holochain relies on different parts of a file from different hosts which are then pieced together from these parts to form a whole *Distributed Hash Table (DHT)*. Every device on the network can function independently, using its own secure ledger of Holochain, only requiring synchronisation of data when necessary or agreed upon by users.

Holochain has a Proof-of-Service consensus system where a user gets rewarded in cryptocurrency when a service is completed on behalf of another user. The cryptocurrency attached to Holochain is called *Holo Token* or *Holo Fuel*. Again Holo Fuel is different to other cryptocurrencies in that it is not a coin nor assigned a monetary value. It is more like a digital bartering system where person A does something for person B and person B could do something in return for an equal exchange, depending upon what they agree upon. Developers will have the capacity to develop their own unique agreement systems or smart contracts.

Ethereum uses *Solidity*, a fairly open ended programming language, allowing developers more freedom in designing their Ethereum based *Dapp* and smart contracts. Unfortunately for developers who have been unable to develop their solutions properly, this has resulted in issues like the *DAO* hack, the *Parity Wallet* hack and other mishaps.

Holochain's DNA and immune system acts as a security measure. If the DNA rules appear to be broken, this information is communicated between the nodes and the perpetrator of the breach is shut out of the Holochain network.

All this technology, whether it is IOTA, Holochain, Hashgraph or similar, is relatively new and evolving but appears to have a bright future. We have seen a large number of changes in just ten years with blockchain and Bitcoin systems. So what may happen in the next ten or twenty years?

6 Digital Currency – Origin and Purpose

Despite the euphoria that appears to surround the rise and fall of Bitcoin, the average person on the street has little idea of Bitcoin and even less idea of other cryptocurrencies. Those that know of Bitcoin and cryptocurrencies claim that it is a new way of life and that the financial world as we know it will be transformed.

Let's look at the history –

Between the early 1990's and 2006 a group of cryptographers called *Cybherpunks* were working on a form of digital currency. Some of the initial prototype digital currencies were: *Digicash, Bitgold*, and *RPOW*. Of this clandestine group, a person named *Satoshi Nakamoto* saw an opportunity during the global financial crisis and introduced a new monetary system called 'Bitcoin'. Satoshi gathered all the ideas of previous forms of digital currency and created a hash-based protocol using a distributed ledger called 'blockchain'. Every transaction is recorded on a blockchain. It cannot be deleted and it is permanent. Every single transaction in the blockchain has a history.

Satoshi hypothesised that it would be hard for Bitcoin to develop in any way which was not interacting with the regular economy.

He was working on an electronic cash system that is fully peer-to-peer with no trusted third party. Blockchain is the infrastructure behind the proposed cryptocurrency.

This new money proposed by Satoshi had some key features:

- accessible 24/7,
- equitable currency,
- digital and encrypted,
- based on mathematics rather than a document vouched by a federal bank,
- no interest accrued,
- minimal transaction fee

It was claimed that Bitcoin had the potential to undermine central authority (governments, institutions) around the world, including the banks. The banks perform an important function in the context of traditional currency including validating currency and to validate actions against frauds. In the case of cryptocurrency, the central authority is being removed. Banks generate profits by charging interest on the money lent to the customers; Bitcoin has no central authority. These concepts are radical features.

Partly due to the cheaper and faster transactions, people have been drawn to cryptocurrencies as they are not tied to any government or geographical area. Therefore they should not be affected by international conflicts or a particular country's status as is the current situation in countries like Ghana and Venezuela. Cryptocurrencies, in theory, are deflationary as their value will naturally increase as more people use the limited supply cryptocoin. However, until such time as all cryptocurrencies are mined, it seems that there is little difference to traditional *fiat* currencies where governments print more money as required.

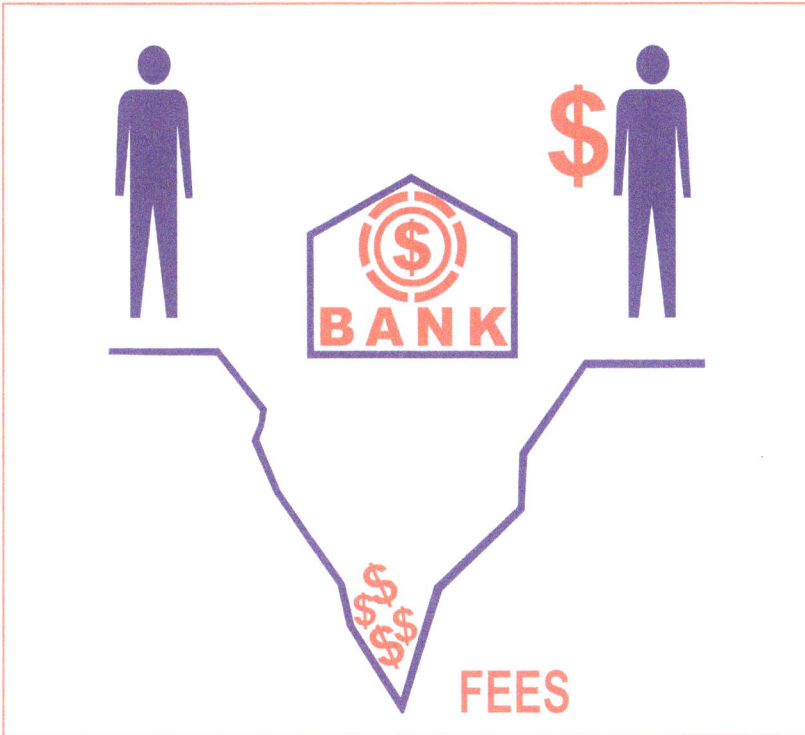

Figure 38: Transaction of funds between individuals and the transaction fee charged by banks (in the current system)

Cryptocurrency is a digital exchangeable currency protected by special methods of data encryption using cryptography. One of the main features of cryptocurrencies is that they operate on a decentralised peer-to-peer network without any government backing or central authority. As an example, if you owned Bitcoin, you could send a friend, or a business that accepts Bitcoin as payment, Bitcoins from your computer without having to go through a third party such as a bank.

The concept of the digital currency has been known since the 1970s. Many of the fiat currencies are digital like Australian dollars, US dollars, and Euros. All these currencies, including digital currencies, are controlled by centralised organisations like the Australian Reserve Bank, the United States Treasury, and so on.

Example: Bitcoin is a cryptocurrency and is a 'network-centric' money. Bitcoin has a decentralised network, an open network and is 'censorship-resistant'.

Digital currency

There has been an unsolved problem in digital currency since the 1990s. The Byzantine problem, or double spending problem, remained until Satoshi Nakamoto claimed to have solved this particular problem by adding a time stamp concept. This ultimately led to the new ideas of blockchain and Bitcoin. The creator has mysteriously remained anonymous since Bitcoin went into circulation in 2009. Although there are many cryptocurrencies in the market now for sale, Bitcoin is the mother of all cryptocurrencies.

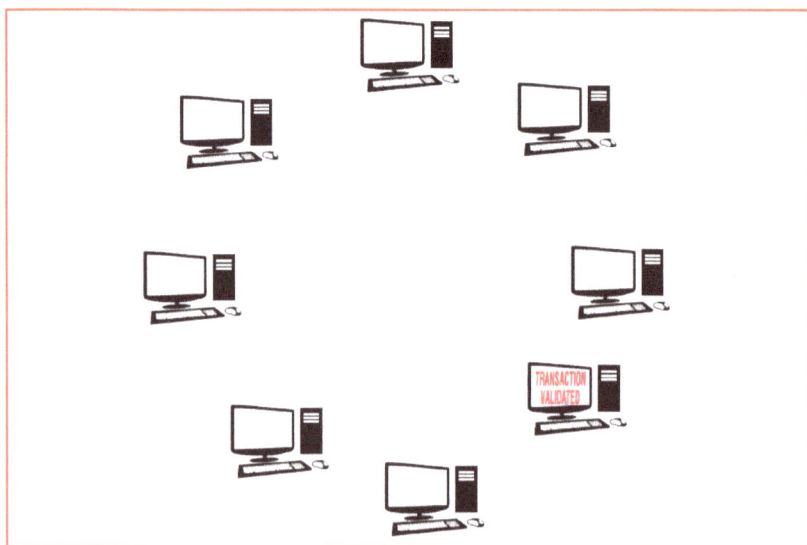

Figure 39: Validation of a transaction in a network by a miner gets rewarded

7   Bitcoin & Other Cryptocurrencies

While the concept of cryptocurrency has been around for some time, its ability to copy data multiple times, reuse and send to multiple people was also its major problem. In 2009, Satoshi Nakamoto in his article titled 'Bitcoin: A Peer-to-Peer Electronic Cash System' proposed a solution to the double spending problem using a peer-to-peer network.

Bitcoin: A Peer-to-Peer Electronic Cash System

Satoshi Nakamoto
satoshin@gmx.com
www.bitcoin.org

Abstract. A purely peer-to-peer version of electronic cash would allow online payments to be sent directly from one party to another without going through a financial institution. Digital signatures provide part of the solution, but the main benefits are lost if a trusted third party is still required to prevent double-spending. We propose a solution to the double-spending problem using a peer-to-peer network. The network timestamps transactions by hashing them into an ongoing chain of hash-based proof-of-work, forming a record that cannot be changed without redoing the proof-of-work. The longest chain not only serves as proof of the sequence of events witnessed, but proof that it came from the largest pool of CPU power. As long as a majority of CPU power is controlled by nodes that are not cooperating to attack the network, they'll generate the longest chain and outpace attackers. The network itself requires minimal structure. Messages are broadcast on a best effort basis, and nodes can leave and rejoin the network at will, accepting the longest proof-of-work chain as proof of what happened while they were gone.

Figure 40: **Abstract of a white paper published by Satoshi Nakamoto**

The issue of double spending has been solved by the blockchain which requires other computers on the network to reach consensus that coin has changed to a new owner. It is also time-stamped.

A simple example of time-stamping is the information on a Microsoft Word document. In a blockchain technology, a similar word document can be copied but it would list all the details including original authors and trails of all copies between then and now. Blockchain technology notarises the information at each and every stage of the transaction by time-stamping.

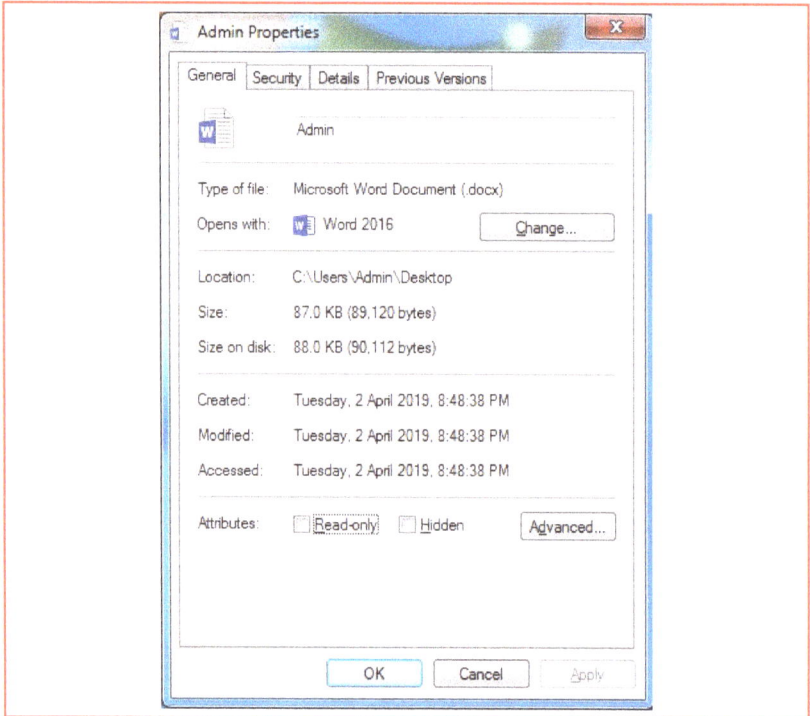

Figure 41: Time-stamping and other features instilled in a typical Microsoft Word document

For some time we have had electronic money (payments) but there have been problems with fraud, conversion of currencies for international transactions, interest payments on transactions and mandatory confirmation by banks. Cryptocurrencies solve most of these problems.

Cryptocurrency is somewhat of a misnomer as very few of what are called cryptocurrencies are actually currencies. The majority of cryptocurrencies could be more accurately broken into various classifications such as commodities, energy or even simply businesses that exist on the blockchain. If we were to look for a blanket coverage, cryptocurrencies may more accurately be described as digital assets. Most cryptocurrencies are built for a specific purpose.

There have been a few thousand cryptocurrencies created since the original Bitcoin and many more are created each year. Of those created, many have since disappeared and many remain niche, leaving only a small proportion as possibly viable.

Any cryptocurrency maintains and increases its value based on how many coins are in use, the legitimacy of the creators of the coin, its transparency, its usability and general popularity.

We will look at some of the current major players and a few of the potential players; although the list is certainly not definitive and we are not recommending any particular coin.

Since the introduction of Bitcoin in 2009, there have been some spinoffs from the Bitcoin blockchain such as *Bitcoin Cash* and *Bitcoin Gold* while others use the same technology such as *Litecoin*. Some have followed *Ethereum* and based their coins on that technology while others have used their own unique programming language. Since anyone can create their own cryptocurrency, most cryptocurrencies will remain niche with only a small number ever likely to become popular and mainstream.

Bitcoin

Of all the cryptocurrencies, Bitcoin is the **King of Crypto** because of its brand recognition. In 2009, Bitcoin became the first cryptocurrency and the name is synonymous with cryptocurrency. Bitcoin may no longer be technically the best option today but, like the iPhone is to smartphone, or Hoover was to vacuum cleaners, (yes, even today, parts of the world still say that they are going to do the hoovering), people will still demand Bitcoin because it is the one that they have heard of and it continues to create headlines. Bitcoin is #1 by ownership, price and usability.

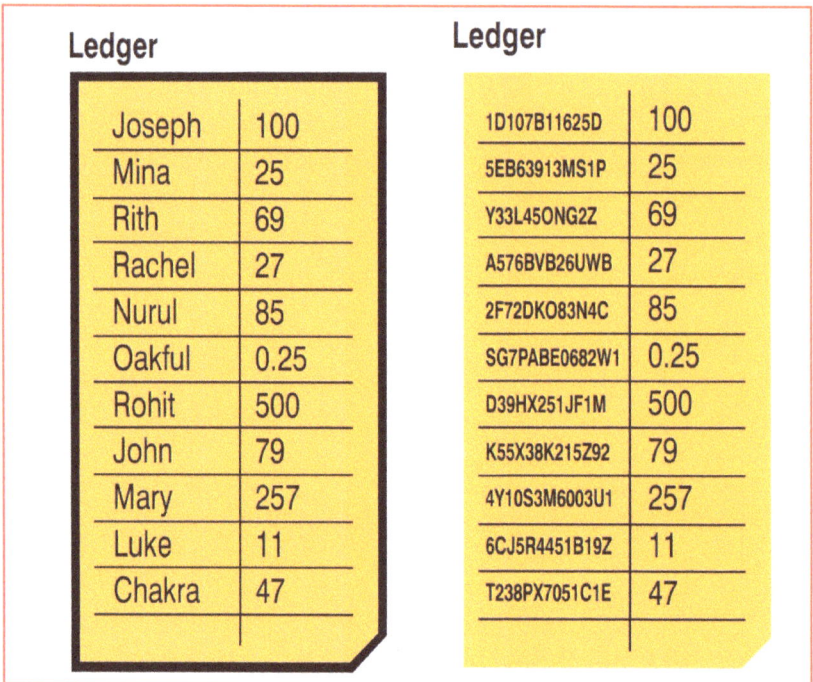

Ledger		Ledger	
Joseph	100	1D107B11625D	100
Mina	25	5EB63913MS1P	25
Rith	69	Y33L45ONG2Z	69
Rachel	27	A576BVB26UWB	27
Nurul	85	2F72DKO83N4C	85
Oakful	0.25	SG7PABE0682W1	0.25
Rohit	500	D39HX251JF1M	500
John	79	K55X38K215Z92	79
Mary	257	4Y10S3M6003U1	257
Luke	11	6CJ5R4451B19Z	11
Chakra	47	T238PX7051C1E	47

Figure 42: Ledger showing a transaction with personal details and encrypted details

Bitcoin and other cyptocurrencies are not owned by, nor controlled by, an organisation; it is based purely on mathematical functions. There is a lack of infrastructure in almost all proprietary technologies that we use including *Facebook, Uber, Whatsapp* and other mobile and web-based applications. There are more custom-designed cryptocurrencies in the market and it will take at least a decade to realise the hidden potential of cryptocurrency in any medium of transaction. Since the inception of Bitcoin, it has physically disappeared from the chart umpteen times (more than 300 times as of Nov 2018). It gained traction when some venture capitalists started showing interest in this product and miners started mining Bitcoins.

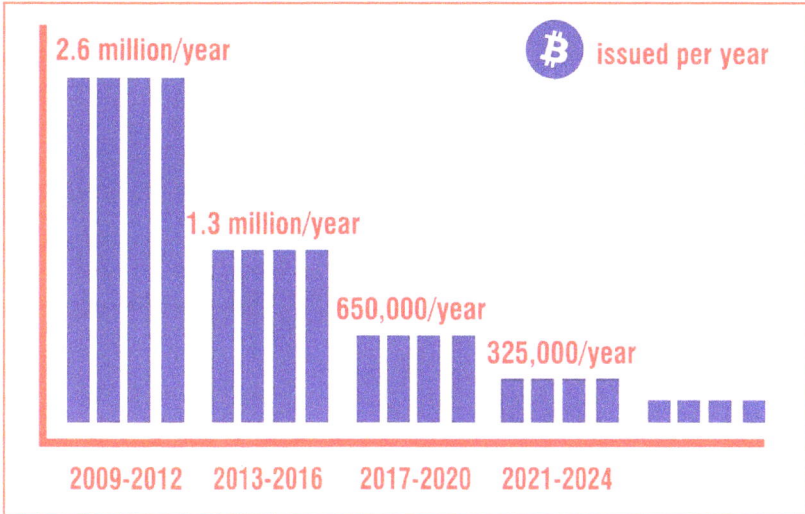

Figure 43: Bitcoins issued per year

The above chart shows that the number of Bitcoins issues has halved every four years since 2009. The anonymity of Satoshi has led to the many people involved in the project adding more ideas and concepts to the basic Bitcoin and associated technology. There were a number of cryptocurrencies evolving in the process with added features like *Smart Contracts, Ether, Ripple* and so on. (See the appendix for acronyms used in the language of cryptocurrency).

Table 7: Timeline of Bitcoin		
Date		**Value (One Bitcoin in $US)**
Early 2009	First Bitcoin is mined	Negligible
Feb 2010	DW Dollar – first Bitcoin exchange	$0.001
May 2010	10,000 Bitcoins spent to buy a pizza worth $25	$0.0025
July 2010	Exchange value of Bitcoin increases ten times	$0.08
April 2011		$1.63
Sep 2012		$12.31
Feb 2013		$30.26
March 2013		$75.00

Imagine 21 million cells on a spreadsheet. (In the case of Bitcoin, there is a maximum of 21 million coins). Each cell, or multiple cell, or fraction of cell, can only be owned by one person at one point in time. Each cell holds information in the Bitcoin network called a public ledger. All cells are homogeneous.

80 per cent of all Bitcoins are already mined. There is no third party managing the transaction of Bitcoins. The reward for checking if the transaction is valid and correct (to avoid double spending) results in the creation of Bitcoin. All miners in the network have to validate the transactions and are awarded a Bitcoin, on average, every 10 minutes. The following tables list values of various denominations of Bitcoin.

Table 8: Denominations of Bitcoin	
Unit	Bitcoin (BTC)
Algorithmic max	20,999,999.9769
MegaBitcoin	1,000,000
KiloBitcoin	1,000
Original block reward	50
DecaBitcoin	10
Bitcoin	1
DeciBitcoin	0.1
CentiBitcoin	0.01
MilliBitcoin	0.001
MicroBitcoin	0.000001
Finney	0.0000001
Satoshi	0.00000001

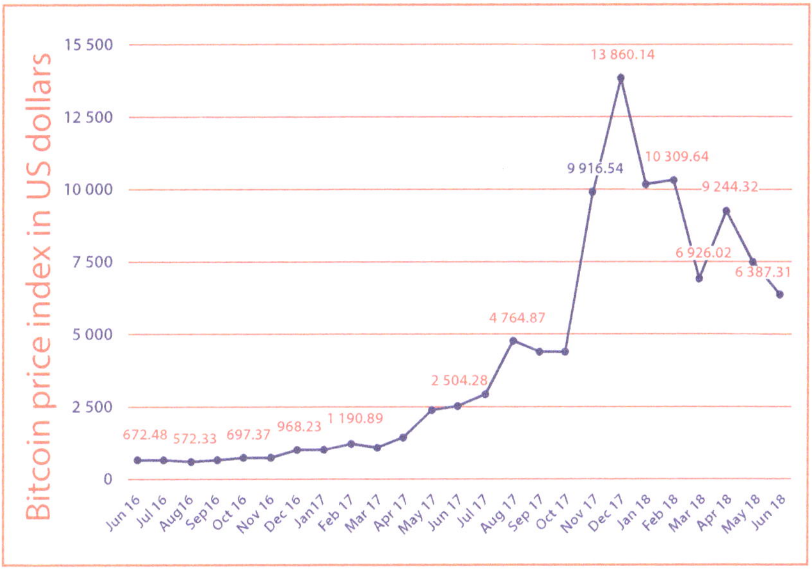

Figure 44: **The price of Bitcoin between June 2016 and July 2018 (in $US)**

Ongoing transactions in the blockchain

Blockchain.info is a Bitcoin block explorer (browser) and wallet for cryptocurrencies like Bitcoin, Bitcoin Cash. The screenshot below is from blockchain.info. Each block shows the number of transactions in each block.

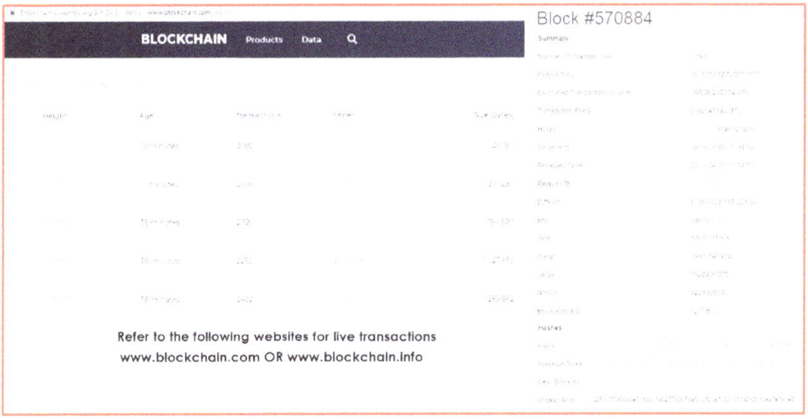

Figure 45: **Screen capture of the latest block from blockchain.info**

The height refers to the block number in the transaction. See *Glossary of Terms* for more details (hash, previous and merkel root).

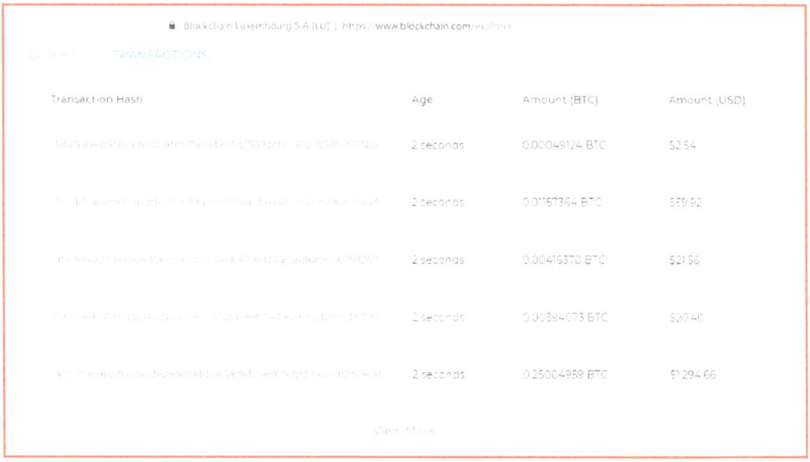

Figure 46: Screen capture showing the number of transactions per day

The hash rate from the above screenshot was 22,125,683.71 terahash per second (TH/s). (One terahash is 10 to the power 12 (10^{12}) hash). In theory, it depends on the number of computers in the cryptocurrency network; with fewer computers working, the easier it is to break. It also depends on the hash function; if it is easily reversible, then anyone can break it.

In Satoshi's article he mentioned that 'the network itself requires minimal structure'. The nodes (individual computers) can leave and rejoin the network at will, accepting the longest proof-of-work chain as proof of what happened while they were away.

Blocks are transactions that are collectively encoded into a single unit and a list of transactions are converted into multiple blocks so that individual computers can handle the encrypting of single blocks.

Longest chain

The longest chain is always considered the valid one; the software always looks for the longest chain. In the following image, what if block 5 was solved exactly at the same time by two people in the node? Then the longest chain will be valid. It will continue to block 6 and so on. The node (miner) that solved block 5 on the shortest chain will not gain any Bitcoins or any form of remuneration.

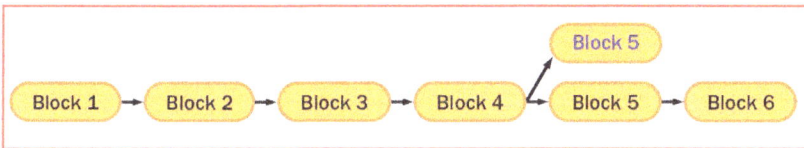

Figure 47: Validation of the longest chain in blockchain protocol

Private key, public key and signature

A private key is a secret and randomly generated number (single 256 bit integer, or 32 bytes) that is known only to the person who generated it. In Bitcoin, the person possessing the private key that corresponds to the funds on the public ledger can spend the funds. A private key is a random number between 1 and 2^{256}. 2^{256} is a large number (it is around 10^{77}), so large that it would take millions of years to guess the key).

A public key is associated with a private key. A public key does not need to be kept secret; it can be calculated from a private key but not the other way round. In Bitcoin, public keys are either compressed or uncompressed. Compressed public keys are 33 bytes and uncompressed public keys are 65 bytes. It is possible to prove that a person knows the private key associated with a public key without divulging the private key. The asymmetric encryption behind the blockchain will allow the user to share one's public key with others and still not risk having their funds stolen.

A signature is a number that proves that a signing operation occurred. A signature is mathematically generated from a hash of something (normally a string, or file, or data) to be signed, plus a private key. With the public key, an algorithm can be used on the signature to determine if the signature was authentically produced from a hash and the private key, without needing to know the private key. Signatures are 73, 72 or 71 bytes long.

How does this private key, public key (base 58) work in Bitcoin?

1. The private key is hashed through the SHA256 algorithm.
2. The result is hashed through RipeDM160. This value is saved and stored as part A or the first part.
3. Part A is hashed through SHA256
4. The process is repeated by hashing it through SHA256
5. A public key is generated (public wallet address base 58)

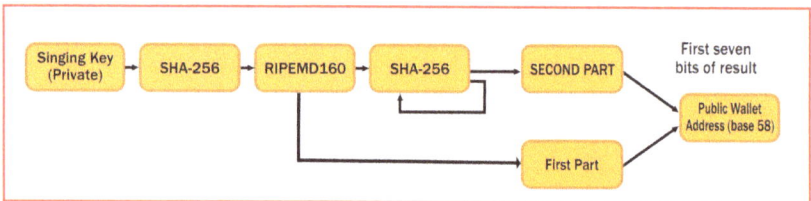

Figure 48: Sequence of steps involved in the generation of public and private keys

In general, alphanumeric characters are 26 English letters, a dozen special characters and ten numerals (0 to 9). A public key is 58 alphanumeric combinations (upper case letters (26) + lower case letters (26) + numerals 0 to 9 (10). Of this total (26 + 26 + 10 = 62 alphanumeric combinations), four characters are avoided as they are ambiguous when printed. Those four characters are zero, upper case "O", upper case "I" (9th letter) and lower case "L" (12th letter). It is designed for manual input copied from some visual source.

A Bitcoin address normally begins with 1 or 3. It is possible to get a Bitcoin address using an account at an online wallet service, or at an exchange that trades cryptocurrency, or via an offline network. It is possible to create a Bitcoin address without an internet connection and it does not require any connection with the Bitcoin network. There is special software available commercially to create a large number of addresses.

A possible Bitcoin address:

123456789ABCDEFGHJKLMNPQRSTUVWXYZabcdefghijkmnopqrst-uvwxyz

Table 9: Alphanumeric combination in a Bitcoin address	
Alphabets	
Lower case	a to z (except lower case L)
Upper case	A to Z (except upper case O and I)
Numbers	Zero

Benefits of blockchain

Each transaction within the ledger is digitally signed thus ensuring its authenticity and high integrity. It has proven to be a reliable platform for the development of contractual and transaction-based uses.

Other cryptocurrencies

Litecoin

Created in 2011by engineer Charlie Lee, Litecoin is often referred to as the little brother of Bitcoin. Some of the major differences between Bitcoin and Litecoin are:

- Litecoin generates blocks four times faster, confirming the legitimacy of transactions quicker and processing a much greater number.

- Litecoin uses an algorithm known as *scrypt* which is memory-intensive compared to the relatively more complex SHA256 used by Bitcoin.
- In mining, the different proof-of-work algorithms means that different hardware is required to produce Bitcoin and Litecoin.
- Litecoin has a limit of 84 million coins compared to Bitcoins 21 million.
- While Litecoin is generally ranked in the top five crypto-currencies by market capitalisation, it is well behind Bitcoin.

Ether

Ether tried to correct some of the main criticisms of Bitcoin especially in terms of security. It has been able to accomplish safer transactions and more flexible contracts that are compatible with any wallet with short block times. There are no limitations or cap for Ether mining as compared to the limitation of bitcoin (21 million bitcoins).

Ethereum allows different developers to raise funds for their own projects and can be a kick-starter for a number of projects.

Dash

Dash was launched in 2014 as an alternative to PayPal and aims to make the technology more approachable for the average consumer.

Monero

Often referred to as the 'privacy coin', Monero transactions are more difficult to track on its blockchain than those of Bitcoin or other cryptocurrencies. Its technology has made it difficult to integrate it into cryptocurrency software and hardware wallets.

OmiseGO

OmiseGo's main purpose is to allow businesses to process payments from a variety of both cryptocurrencies and fiat currencies quickly and affordably. It is already implemented in some Asian countries and some major businesses like McDonalds. It's based on the Ethereum blockchain and technology.

Ripple

It was developed about six years ago and aimed at the financial sector. Ripple already has over 75 major financial institutions such as Westpac, American Express and UBS working with the Ripple blockchain solution. The aim is to increase security and transaction speeds for international money transfers while reducing the associated fees. Ripple soared 1000 per cent between December 2017 and January 2018 and then fell as traders took their profits.

While other cryptocurrencies are designed to be deregulated, decentralised and anonymous means of transferring funds, Ripple is centralised and all transactions on the network can be tracked from the beginning to the end point.

Another major difference between Bitcoin and Ripple is that Ripple allows users to transact in fiat currency like US dollars, Euro and Pound Sterling as well as cryptocurrency.

Zcash

Zcash aspires to become a mainstream payment option for users as it provides more security and privacy than Bitcoin. Unfortunately, it seems that people are preferring to use Monero when seeking better security and privacy features.

Steem

Steemit is a decentralised blogging and publishing platform which enables authors of original content to receive compensation from readers and users based on the user's rating of such content. Steem is the cryptocurrency used to reward users for posting, commenting, voting and sharing content on Steemit.

Bitcoin Cash

This cryptocurrency resulted from disagreements within the Bitcoin community regarding issues of scalability and how to handle its rapid growth. It is a completely separate cryptocurrency from Bitcoin. Since its creation in August 2017, there has been controversy as some prominent influencers and websites have knowingly misled customers by saying Bitcoin Cash is Bitcoin. Some more reputable organisations are referring to Bitcoin Cash as BCash to reduce or avoid the confusion. To add to the potential confusion, Bitcoin Cash is supported on many Bitcoin ATMs. Bitcoin Cash has been heavily promoted at cryptocurrency events and televised interviews with industry insiders.

As might be expected, individuals and companies are buying Bitcoin Cash instead of their intended purchase of Bitcoin and have lost their funds.

Bitcoin Gold

The intention of Bitcoin Gold, when created in October 2017, was to make mining more affordable for the average person. The reward for any mining is Bitcoin Gold not Bitcoin. There is no association with Bitcoin apart from its use of the Bitcoin name for credibility.

Bitcoin Diamond

Created in November 2017, it is being promoted as the new version of Bitcoin. It promised cheaper transaction fees and improved privacy. However, investors are very cautious as its development team is completely anonymous, the source code is not being provided, and all its social media accounts were created in the month that it was created. (Refer to the section on *Hacks and Scams*).

Peercoin

Peercoin is also known as PP Coin or PPC. It utilises both proof-of-stake and proof-of-work systems. One of the main goals when it was conceptualised in 2013 was to alleviate the extremely large amount of electrical energy required to power the Bitcoin network.

Feathercoin

This was created circa 2013 as a spinoff from Litecoin. While it offered little in uniqueness, it is still active but with only a small trading volume.

Feathercoin utilises the hashing *NeoScrypt* algorithm which is not as complex as the SHA256 used by Bitcoin. Feathercoin's key attribute is that it takes about a minute to generate a block while confirming transactions in about one-tenth of the time it takes on the Bitcoin blockchain. The reward, to be distributed among the miners who solve it, is 40 coins per block. The maximum number of Feathercoins that can be produced is 336 million compared to 84 million for Litecoin.

Dogecoin

It was introduced in December 2013 as a joke currency but is now a rapidly growing form of digital currency. It can be used to buy goods and services, or trade it for other currencies, but one of the most popular uses for Dogecoin is 'tipping' social media users who provide interesting and noteworthy content.

As of February 2018, it is reported that there are over 113 billion coins that have been mined. Its hash function is based on Scrypt.

Golem

This utilises an Ethereum-based transaction system to settle payments between providers, requestors and software developers. Golem enables users and applications (requestors) to rent out cycles of other users' machines (providers). Any users, ranging from single personal computer owners to large data centres, can share resources through Golem and they get paid in *Golem Network Tokens (GNT)* by the requestor.

SALT

SALT is a loan platform where users can deposit various cryptocurrencies and in return receive a real world money loan.

NEO

Neo is a Chinese-based cryptocurrency that has survived China's changing stances on cryptocurrency and stands to benefit from China's huge population.

IOTA

IOTA is a public distributed ledger that stores transactions in a *Directed Acyclic Graph (DAG)* structure called a *Tangle*. The Tangle is used in place of the blockchain structure commonly used by other cryptocurrencies like Bitcoin. It has created a marketplace for providing and selling data.

EOS

EOS promises to process payments without charging any fees and is a direct competitor to Ethereum.

Stellar

Stellar aims to revolutionise the banking industry with faster and cheaper international payments using an open-sourced blockchain.

TRON / Tronix

Tron aims to decentralise entertainment by offering a distribution method that benefits both creator, by protecting copyright, and consumers by reducing costs. Tronix is the cryptocurrency that will allow the purchase of content and services on the network.

Civic

This is a secure identity database with the potential to create a global database for storing and sharing personal and medical data in a secure and decentralised way.

BitConnect

Bitconnect has a large market cap and through *BCCPay* debit card allows BitConnect Coin and Bitcoin to make payments via the Mastercard network.

8   Initial Coin Offerings

What is an Initial Coin Offering?

An Initial Coin Offering (ICO) is a fundraising method in which new projects trade their future crypto tokens for cryptocurrencies like Bitcoin and Ether which have an immediate liquid value. An ICO is somewhat similar to an Initial Public Offering (IPO) in which investors purchase shares of a company. Unlike the purchase of shares, the majority of ICO tokens do not come with any entitlements of ownership, voting rights, or a share in future profits. Generally, a percentage of the tokens are sold to participants in the ICO and a percentage is retained for the future needs of the company such as private investors. The companies set the terms of the ICO so there are no standard requirements. Both large and small investors participate in funding projects through an ICO. In Australia, companies seeking to raise funds by units in a trust, or securities in a company, are generally required to provide a disclosure statement such as a prospectus or Product Disclosure Statement (PDS). These are to assist what is termed 'non-sophisticated investors' make an informed decision about the investment's risks and possible returns. A prospectus includes any significant tax implications of the investment.

Some product disclosure statements issued for ICOs may not comply with Australian requirements and therefore offer no protection under Australian law. Some unscrupulous ICO operators issue a fake prospectus and most of these ICOs turn out to be scams.

The Australian Investment and Securities Commission (ASIC) has a register to enable prospective investors to check whether the ICO issuer is a company registered in Australia by undertaking an organisation and business name search. The ASIC website also enables investors to search the *Australian Financial Services*

Licensee register to check whether an ICO issuer has a licence in Australia.

ICO fund raising may not require a disclosure statement if the cryptocurrency being offered has the same characteristics as Bitcoin because Bitcoin is not considered a security nor a financial product in Australia. Companies are using cryptocurrencies to raise capital for a project but, if they subsequently make further developments or improvements, it may change the characteristics of the original project and be subject to Corporations Tax and potentially Capital Gains Tax (CGT). Most digital currencies provide a white paper that sets out the basic technical specifications of the cryptocurrency. ICO tokens do not provide the diversification that most serious investors seek regardless of how many different tokens are purchased. As there is no real underlying value with any of the tokens, the value of the token fluctuates due to popularity and their values rise and fall together even if their associated projects are unrelated.

How to evaluate an ICO

It is impossible to say with any certainty that an ICO will be successful but there are a number of issues that a potential investor should consider before investing.

Firstly, who are the individuals that make up the development team and advisory board? What experience have they had with other cryptocurrencies and are there any famous or high profile people lending their name to the ICO? Research *Facebook, LinkedIn, Google* and other social media sites.

Similarly, the project should be researched using cryptocurrency forums like *Bitcointalk*. Yes, there can be many pages on a thread but it is important to read and understand what is being said or, equally, not said. Red flags should be raised if a developer is not answering certain questions raised by investors or is absent from the forum. Many forums contain rank and activity degree messages and this again will provide a knowledgeable reader with an indication of how seriously to take comments. Newcomers and lowly-ranked writers would be taken less seriously than experienced writers. The forum search facilities should be used to seek out words such as 'scam', 'con', 'hack', etc.

Bounty posts on *Reddit, Twitter, Facebook* and similar social media should (generally) not be treated seriously as these posts are purely to generate hype regarding the project. Bounty threads often provide some reward to users for spreading positive information about the project and some investors participate in return for tokens.

As with Initial Public Offerings (IPOs) for shares, only a small fraction of the ICOs will make any money; most will disappear.

Possibly the most successful ICO to date has been *Tezos* which raised $232 million in less than a month. There have also been some major frauds and hacks such as the *Mycelium ICO* where the team members disappeared with the funds raised and the *CoinDash ICO* where $7 million was stolen when their website was hacked and the ICO wallet address was changed to the hacker's address.

9   Buying, Storage and Security

There are three ways of acquiring cryptocurrencies. Firstly, for those that participate in mining, they will receive some cryptocurrency if they are successful in processing the transaction on the cryptocurrency blockchain.

Most people will purchase their Bitcoin or other cryptocurrency online through exchanges. Before purchasing any cryptocurrency, one needs to understand <u>why</u> it is being purchased. The mining system of the cryptocurrency needs to be checked as this can directly affect the prices. For example, news of an upcoming switch from proof-of-work to proof-of-stake might lead to an increase in price as people start buying the coins to use in the mining process. Also, higher mining rewards can lead to inflation and a declining coin value. If coins are being purchased to buy goods and services, then an established currency like Bitcoin is appropriate. For investment purposes, buying across a range of cryptocurrencies is likely to improve overall returns and minimise risk

To buy, store or send cryptocurrency, an encrypted digital wallet is required. Misnomers are common and the term wallet is no different. Because we are dealing with digital currency, there is no physical currency that is actually kept in the wallet. The cryptocurrency wallets, or wallets for short, are software programs that run on a computer and provide access to any one, or sometimes multiple, cryptocurrencies. is the wallet must be compatible with the currency being purchased. The wallet can connect with, and analyse, the blockchain, allowing you to send and receive currency with other users of that blockchain. Blockchain is simply a ledger containing the entire history of a cryptocurrency. To prevent tampering, most blockchains are open source and decentralised.

Each wallet has a private and a public key. Each key is a seemingly random string of numbers and letters. The public key can be likened to a bank account number so it is the address given to other people who are going to deposit cryptocurrency to a wallet. To authorise this transfer, the private key is used which is similar to a PIN or password. Like a password, it is important that is remains secret and secure. A Bitcoin private key randomly generated by the Bitcoin algorithm can be up to 50 characters long so it needs to be stored securely on a laptop, storage device, USB stick or paper. Back-up is also important, offsite or in the cloud.

There are a variety of wallets, hot and cold, hard and soft. There are basically five types, each providing different levels of ease of use and security. Hot wallets are those connected to the internet, using download software programs for a computer or phone. A cold wallet is when the storage is offline.

Firstly, online wallets from exchanges or a third party organisation run in the cloud and are easy to setup and use. However, being cloud-based, they are the least secure and are the ones that are targeted when the exchanges are hacked. To access, some only require an email address and password while the more secure ones may require scans of a passport or other identification for verification. Most secure are online services that provide 2FA – two factor authentication. Advantages of the cloud base are that the servers are more secure than most personal computers, they cannot be lost and they are accessible from any computer with an internet connection. Depending on the wallet used, some will take either a flat fee or a percentage for every transaction made.

Secondly, a digital wallet can be created on a computer or phone for storage of cryptocurrency. These desktop wallets are easy to install and maintain and are available for Windows, Mac and Linux although some may be limited to a particular operating system. For added security, off–line is preferred. The disadvantages of desktop wallets are that they require strong malware, anti-virus software and firewall.

Thirdly, there are apps that can run on smartphones. The smartphone wallets have similar advantages and disadvantages to the desktop wallet but with the added advantage of being able to scan a QR code for other wallet addresses for faster transactions. A major disadvantage is that if a smartphone is lost or stolen, a person who can gain access to the phone may also gain access to the funds.

Next there are hardware wallets such as a specially-designed piece of hardware or a USB stick to keep the private key. These provide added security as the user plugs the device in, logs into the computer, makes the transaction, and then unplugs. As with any hardware like a USB stick, one needs to back up regularly and store it securely.

A paper wallet can also be created whereby the wallet's public and private key are printed and filed in a safe or secure filing cabinet. Unfortunately paper wallets are the most complex but offer a very high level of security. The user is required to generate their own keys and need a key generator or software wallet to work. Transfer of currency requires two steps: transfer to a software wallet and then from the software wallet to the recipient.

Some wallets have additional features like checking live exchange rates with the fiat currency of choice.

Which wallet is best will be a personal choice but when choosing a wallet, it is often best to use one of the most popular wallets such as *Bitcoin Core, blockchain wallet, MyEther wallet, Ledger Nano S wallet, TREZOR wallet or KeepKey wallet* to name a few.

At this point, it may be timely to remind the user of basic but often overlooked practices regarding computers and smartphones. Strong usernames and passwords should be used and kept secure. Passwords for cryptocurrency should not be used on any other websites. Anti-virus and anti-malware software must be installed and kept up to date and a secure firewall set up.

Software should not be installed from companies you don't trust and only verified and trusted wallets should be used. When software updates for the wallet are received, the update should be carried out as soon as possible. Online wallets should not be accessed from public Wi-Fi.

Because it is almost impossible to get any currency back if sent in error, a public address should be double-checked when giving it to a user who is sending currency. To maximise the security of a private key, it should not be stored on a computer or online.

Most people purchase their cryptocurrency through exchanges. Australia has a number of exchanges but they charge a premium price therefore many Australian investors will sign up to overseas exchanges where they can buy for a better price.

To purchase cryptocurrency is relatively easy and involves verifying one's identity on the exchange, depositing fiat currency such as the dollar or Euro as payment and then buying the coin.

Since the first Bitcoin ATM was opened in Vancouver, Canada in October 2013, Bitcoin ATM's are being installed in many of the major cities around the world. These ATMs allow users to purchase Bitcoin and a limited number of other currencies like Litecoin and Ethereum through the ATM. The ATM allows the purchase of Bitcoin by depositing money into the machine and, if needed, withdrawal of cash from the machine by converting Bitcoin into traditional currency. Two issues that users need to be aware of are the lower conversion rates and much higher fees than through online services.

Examples of Security Lapses

In around 2013, a crypto investor named James Howells threw out a hard drive containing Bitcoin private keys to Bitcoin worth about $79 million. James is not alone as there is an estimated $33 billion worth of Bitcoin lost forever because retrieval codes have gone missing, or the owners have died without notifying next of kin of the existence of Bitcoin or the codes to retrieve the Bitcoin. Another in XRP cryptocurrency worth an estimated one billion dollars belonged to Matthew Mellon who died in Mexico on 16 April 2018. His family reportedly (the family have denied this) had been unable to locate the codes needed to retrieve his fortune. Another person attempted to do the correct thing and split the code between himself and his business partner. Unfortunately his business partner died and there was no backup so about 500 Bitcoins, worth at the time around $5.3 million, were lost forever.

As mentioned previously in this book, Satoshi Nakamoto, Bitcoin creator, vanished in 2010 and none of the 1 million coins he reportedly mined have moved since that time. This has raised speculation that Nakamoto may have lost his private key or that he may have died or committed suicide and failed to pass on his private key details to next of kin.

10   Purchasing Goods and Services

The first purchase recorded using cryptocurrency was for a pizza where the person wishing to purchase it offered to pay 10,000 Bitcoins. The person received the pizza and transferred the Bitcoins. Based upon current values, that was probably the most expensive pizza ever purchased.

Compared to some other countries, Australia may be a little slow in purchasing goods and services using cryptocurrencies. There are some shops that will allow payment in cryptocurrencies but many of these are for small purchases like a cup of coffee. Prior to the price collapse of Bitcoin in January 2018, some vendors were willing to accept Bitcoins as part-payment for the sale of their houses. It was possibly just a good marketing ploy because these advertisements disappeared quickly in January 2018. In Queensland, business operators in the small township of *Agnes Waters* have banded together to accept Bitcoin but, again, this may be a public relations exercise.

In Australia, it is currently impractical to do everyday shopping using cryptocurrencies. One online business of Satoshi called *Living Room* allows customers to use 11 different cryptocurrencies to pay their household bills providing they have BPAY facilities like ANZ Bank and Australia Post.

Power Ledger is an Australian-based energy trading platform that enables buyers and sellers to trade renewable energy without the need for an intermediary.

If we look at what is happening overseas, we may get a glimpse of where Australia may be heading.

In the USA, Bitcoin and some other cryptocurrencies can be used to purchase a variety of goods from gift cards to airfares but there are restrictions.

Three companies that most Australians will be familiar with are *Microsoft, Expedia* and, for accountants and bookkeepers, *Intuit* (more commonly known as *QuickBooks*).

Microsoft allows customers to use Bitcoin to deposit funds into their Microsoft account. Once deposited, the Bitcoin funds are non-refundable. The funds can then only be used to purchase games, movies and apps in the Windows and Xbox stores but not for any purchases from the Microsoft online store.

Since June 2014, *Expedia* customers have had the option to pay for their hotel bookings with Bitcoins but only for hotel bookings and not for airline bookings.

As part of its *QuickBooks Online* electronic invoicing, small businesses can accept cryptocurrency payments through *Intuit*. There is normally a fee associated with cryptocurrency payments.

There are at least two companies – *eGifter* and *Gyft* – that accept payment in Bitcoin when gift cards are purchased. This allows the purchaser / user of these gift cards to make purchases in the gift card stores that don't accept payment in cryptocurrency.

Shopify is an ecommerce platform that allows merchants to sell their products through their own online shop, similar to *EBay*. Since about November 2013, Shopify merchants have had the option to accept Bitcoin payments.

There is also a chain of jewellery shops, a satellite television and internet provider, airline flights through a company called Cheap Air, and pizza delivery that allow such payments.

In the UK, there are reports of houses being purchased with Bitcoin.

Shops that accept cryptocurrency as payment generally have some signage such as 'Bitcoin accepted here' to advertise that they accept cryptocurrency. Generally, the accepted cryptocurrency is limited to just Bitcoin and maybe one or two of the major cryptocurrencies. Similarly, for online shopping, whether Bitcoin or other cryptocurrencies are accepted is normally listed as an available payment option in the shopping cart or in the 'frequently asked questions' on the site.

There are also a number of online business directories such as *SpendBitcoins* and *CoinMap* that help locate local business and restaurants that accept cryptocurrencies.

In Australia, *Living Room* of Satoshi enables Australians to pay bills using Bitcoin and a few other cryptocurrencies.

Fees Involved

One problem with Bitcoin payments is the surcharges and the fact that the precise amount is unknown to the customer until after the transaction is finalised. A software engineer, James Zaki, wanted to try purchasing a beer with Bitcoin. In cash, the beer was going to cost $7 but after completing his Bitcoin transaction for the purchase, the beer had cost $11.61: a 66 per cent surcharge. The surcharge is basically a mining fee.

BitRocket is a cryptocurrency ATM operator in Australia. Its rates change constantly and are based on Australian prices such as *BTCMarkets.net* and *Independent Reserve.com* with approximately 5.5 per cent being added to the total.

While Bitcoin and a small number of other cryptocurrencies like *Litecoin* and *Ethereum* are starting to gain a foothold as a currency of exchange, they still have a long way to go. There is a major reliance on such things as debit cards loaded with Bitcoin to make traditional payments and the rollout of the Bitcoin ATM is very slow. This means that, for most people, it is not a convenient way to exchange Bitcoin or a few other cryptocurrencies for traditional cash to pay for everyday goods and services like groceries, doctor or dental bills.

In Australia, it is likely that the clientele of a business may influence whether Bitcoin or any cryptocurrency is accepted. Businesses in areas dominated by Gen Y and millennials may be more likely to benefit from accepting Bitcoin as a method of payment.

11 Mining and Trading

The issuance of cryptocurrencies is carried out through a process called 'mining'. The use of this term and an analogy with mineral mining may not be accidental.

Theoretically, anyone with a computer could mine cryptocurrencies and it was extremely easy to do when Bitcoin first began. Today, the reality is that super-fast computers with large computational capacities and specialised software, as well as a source of low-cost electricity, are required and so mining is now out of the realm of the home computer.

Today, the majority of mining is normally done in a pool. A pool is a service combining the capacities of different computers for more efficient mining of the cryptocurrency. If successful in solving the equation, each pool-user shares in the reward, proportionally to the work undertaken. This comes down to chance. If there are 100 miners, then a miner has a one per cent chance of mining the next block.

These specialised computers – usually desktops rather than laptop computers – used solely for mining have increased the difficulty of earning a Bitcoin. The currency automatically regulates the difficulty of the mathematical problem by adding complexity to the hash value which computers need to find, as well as the number of Bitcoins a miner receives as a reward. The reward is often newly-created coins of the type mined or a transaction fee payable by everyone whose transaction was packaged into the newly-mined block. If a large number of miners are connected to the network, the difficulty of solving a block increases but decreases as less miners seek new Bitcoins. This is known as the hash rate.

The miners use special software to solve cryptocurrency algorithms using a computer that has a high powered graphical user interface or graphics card. With Bitcoin mining, the most important component of the computer is the graphics card or graphics processing unit. This takes a lot of energy and also emits lots of heat. (See *hashing* for more details).

Cryptocurrency, once mined, is not visible except on computer and tablet screens. Similar to limited resources like gold, cryptocurrency has a cap on it. Bitcoin, the original cryptocurrency, has a maximum limit of 21 million.

Figure 49: Transaction of a Bitcoin in a computer

Bitcoin mining is a specialised algorithm system that is made to hash blocks with incredible efficiency in terms of protection but it uses a huge amount of electricity. Bitcoin miners collect all loose transactions (transfer, payment, gift...) on the network and they line them up in sequence. The miners will use an SHA256 algorithm to create, digest, and then take those to create more digest and it will all come to a final digest. The miners also time-stamp transactions during the mining process.

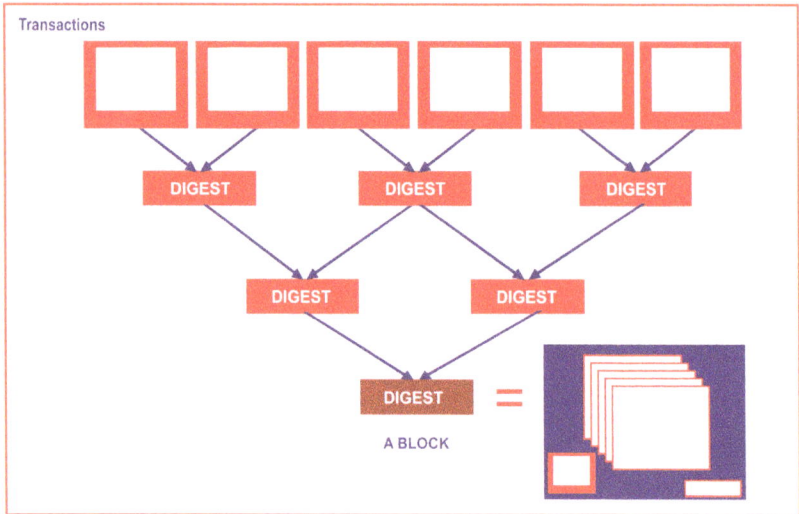

Figure 50: **Schematics of the transactions and digestion of a block (hence the named blockchain)**

Block data is something that is provided by the user (general public). A block is generated from the hash of the previous block and creates index, hash, data and time-stamp. Miners line up the blocks in order and they are connected to each other. Each block includes details of the previous block, nonce and a few transactions.

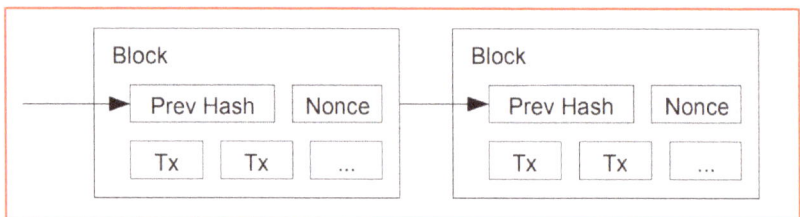

Figure 51: **Excerpt from Satoshi's white paper showing block, previous hash and nonce**

The input of the current transaction (block) has to be the output of the previous transaction; it is sequential. There was always some anonymity in the transactions; the address is new and refreshed for every transaction. This was part of the original source code.

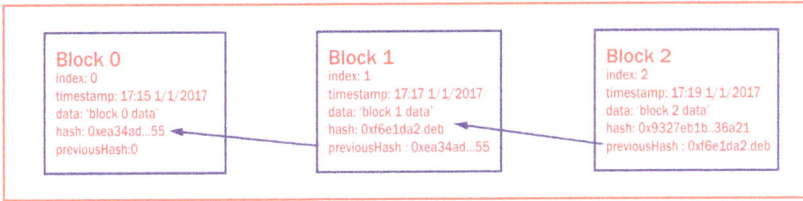

Figure 52: Interconnection of blocks in a transaction

Creation of a new block in the system

Once a new block is created in a system, the block is sent to everyone in the network. Each node then verifies the block and adds the block onto the chain. A consensus is made among all the nodes; the nodes agree about which blocks are valid and which are not.

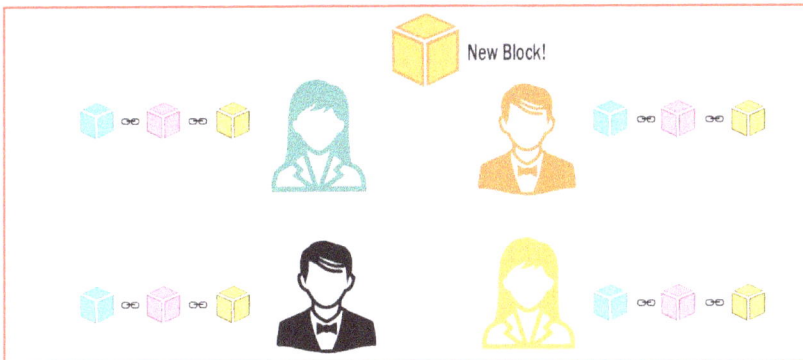

Figure 53: Creation of a new block in a system

Figure 54: Addition of that new block in the system

Figure 55: **Consensus of that new block in the system**

Timestamp

A time-stamp server is built into each and every transaction. It is like notarising every transaction. Blockchain technology notarises the information at each and every stage of transaction by a technique called 'time-stamping'.

All the current transactions are incorporated into one file and hashed along with all other transactions. This gives one hash output. It combines with the next block of transactions then hashed again. This hash output is going to be the same as long as the historical transactions are the same. This is the core logic behind the trustworthiness of the blockchain.

The timestamp proves that the data must have existed at the time, obviously, in order to get into the hash. Each timestamp includes the previous timestamp in its hash, forming a chain, with each additional timestamp reinforcing the ones before it.

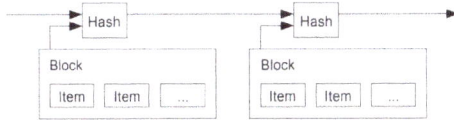

Figure 56: Timestamp of each block in a chain

An example of the concept is the general information on a Microsoft Word document as follows:

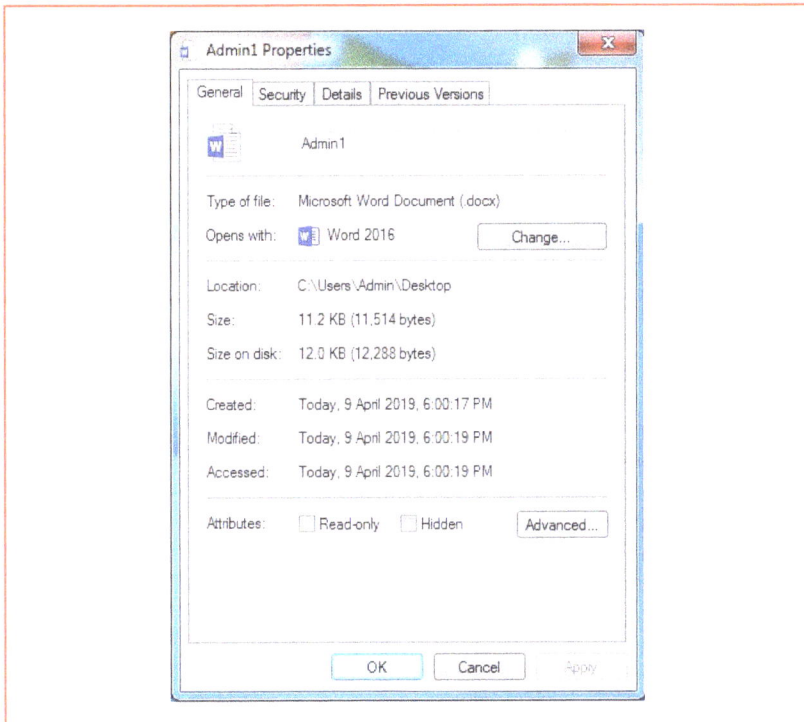

Figure 57: Example of time-stamping using a Microsoft Word document

The above Word document, as with a ledger, can be altered by a person or user that has access to the security settings to edit, control, and modify the document. If this document was in a blockchain network, then any change made by the user will need to be verified / validated by all users on the network and full transparency is thus achieved.

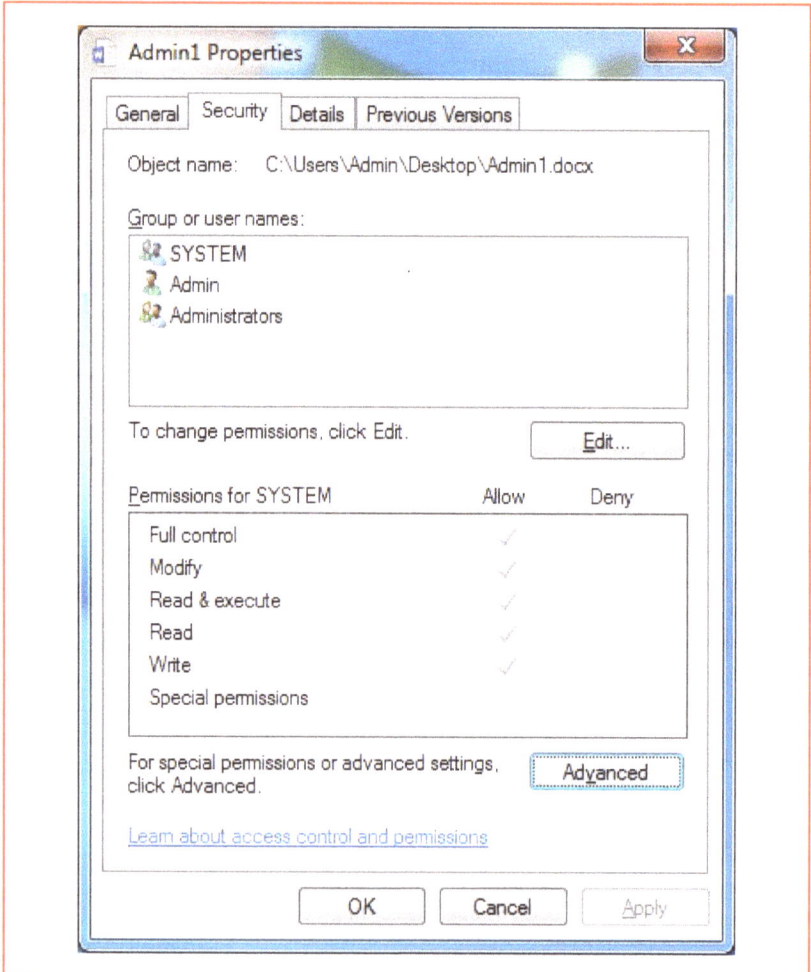

Figure 58: Security settings and permission details on a Microsoft document

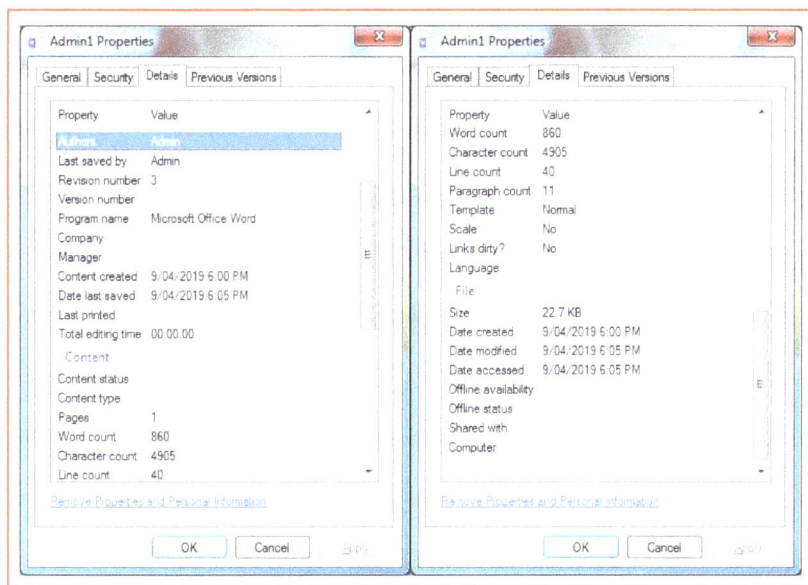

Figure 59: **Description, origin, file details and status of a Microsoft Word document**

In blockchain technology, this document can be copied but it would list all the details including original authors and trails of all users copied since it was created. If the content of a Word document is transferred into another Word document situated in the same, or a new, operating system, the date of creation, modification, and author details can be easily erased. This erasure of trails is not possible in a blockchain technology because of the basic protocol behind the system. Different cryptocurrencies have very different mining systems but two of the most popular are proof-of-work and proof-of-stake.

Proof-of-work

This is the type of system used by Bitcoin. A block is encoded with all the previous blocks attached to it and then the miners take the encoding of the whole blockchain and feed it into an SHA256 algorithm with some random numbers (nonces). The miners want to return a value with a low number of zeros because the more leading zeros required, the harder the mining becomes.

In 2009 and 2010, the number of zero bits were smaller as the number of computers involved in mining was less. As the network increases in size, the algorithm makes the steps to reach a solution tougher by increasing the number of zeros required to do this.

Proof-of-Work

The proof-of-work involves scanning for a value that when hashed, such as with SHA-256, the hash begins with a number of zero bits. The average work required is exponential in the number of zero bits required and can be verified by executing a single hash.

For our timestamp network, we implement the proof-of-work by incrementing a nonce in the block until a value is found that gives the block's hash the required zero bits. Once the CPU effort has been expended to make it satisfy the proof-of-work, the block cannot be changed without redoing the work. As later blocks are chained after it, the work to change the block would include redoing all the blocks after it.

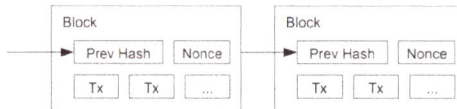

Figure 60: Proof of work mentioned by Satoshi on his paper

The miners look for a specific number of zeros (40s in 2018) by hashing the previous hash (the file that represents all the transactions) by incrementing nonce (number used once) and seeing how much time it takes to make the new transaction into a number beginning with a number of zero bits. Some 'magic nonce' create 40 plus zeros. (Hash rate is the number of combination guesses per second).

Miners work towards solving the block and this only happens statistically once every ten minutes. As more and more mining power enters the network, the rate at which new blocks are found is going to be less than 10 minutes (possibly 8 or 9 minutes). However, the code self-regulates automatically to add more zeros required to be found by miners and that brings the rate back to one Bitcoin generated every ten minutes.

Once a transaction has occurred in a node, the transaction details are wrapped in a cryptographic digital signature and then sent off to the Bitcoin network. The Bitcoin network is made up of user-controlled special computers that verify transactions by performing difficult cryptographic functions. The computer's hardware that runs the network verifies transactions and performs cryptographic functions. The receiver has to wait optimistically for some time for the transaction because the miners have to do their job.

For Bitcoin, there are over 85,000 nodes across the world (as of November 2018). If someone was to tamper with the blockchain (Bitcoin) and be accepted by everyone else, then the hacker would need to tamper with all the blocks on the chain, redo the proof-of-work for each block and take control of more than 50% of the peer-to-peer network. It is impossible to do.

Ethereum will be switching from proof-of-work to proof-of-stake. This mining system requires coin owners to hold special wallets holding coins online. The coins in the wallet then automatically interface with the network and mine new blocks. It is a relatively efficient way of mining but also relatively complicated and can result in an unusual hoarding of coins.

Table 10: Levels of trust associated with the different commodities	
Commodity	Trust
Gold	Something
Bank notes (fiat currency)	Someone – Central authority (government-backed)
Digital	Individual (decentralised and distributed)

The value of gold that hedges world economy is around nine trillion dollars. It takes $100 to $150 to produce an ounce of gold (28.35 grams). As of Feb 2018, a gram of gold is worth about $55.

An ounce (28.35 grams) = 28.35 * 55 = $1559.25

The difference in value ($1559.25 – $150 = $1409.25) is imputed or, in other words, the value assigned by the market of demand and supply. Gold is a limited commodity.

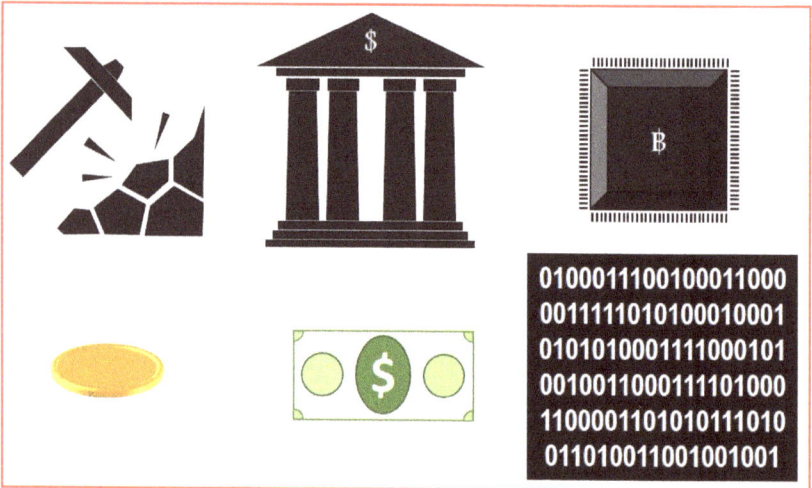

Figure 61: Medium of transaction – gold, paper and computer

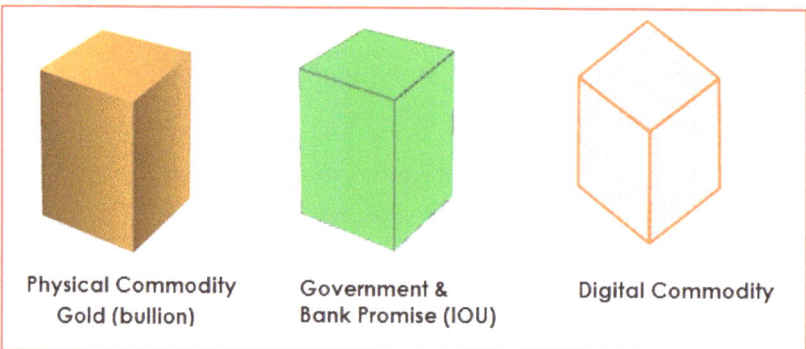

| Physical Commodity Gold (bullion) | Government & Bank Promise (IOU) | Digital Commodity |

Figure 62: Money – commoditised trust (gold, fiat currency and cryptocurrency based on something, government and mathematics respectively)

The blockchain encryption has a unique ability to track every transaction of cryptocurrency. Cryptocurrencies, like Bitcoin, are trackable to their origin including the time of mining. This trackability as to ownership and transparency is not possible with fiat currency nor a gold bar. A dollar bill could belong to anyone in the world and it is not designed to be trackable.

Despite all their potential applications, the main reason many people are buying cryptocurrencies is as an investment. However, cryptocurrencies are speculative and involve significant risks: highly volatile, vulnerable to hacking and capital losses and sensitive to secondary activity. Choosing the right cryptocurrency could see significant capital gains but, as with any investment, research is critical. The waters can always be tested with a small amount of money before committing larger sums.

In December 2017, the *Chicago Board Options Exchange* began trading futures contracts on Bitcoin. (In the past, the *Winklevoss* twins, who own large amounts of Bitcoin, tried unsuccessfully to create their own exchange-traded fund). Many large Wall Street brokerage and clearing houses are not allowing customers to trade Bitcoin futures and some others are placing restrictions on the margins a trader can use for Bitcoin futures or limiting the amount that can be purchased.

It is inevitable that other futures exchanges will allow trading in futures contracts in Bitcoin and other better known crypto-currencies.

12   Hacking and Scams

Cryptocurrencies have been described as the 'Wild West'– it is unregulated and full of scams, fraud, theft and danger; but at the same time, it is a market full of opportunities. It has been said that there is no asset class in the world that is as volatile and risky.

It has not all been plane sailing for Bitcoin from the beginning. The Bitcoin world has been plagued by hacks, scams and abusive practices and, today, cryptocurrencies are attracting the attention of more scammers. As far as is known, the Bitcoin software has not been hacked; the hacking has been aimed at the related services such as exchanges.

The first vulnerability in the Bitcoin protocol was found in August 2010. Transactions had not been checked for over 24 hours and, during this period, an unlimited amount of Bitcoin was created. On 15 August, there was one large transfer of Bitcoin which was discovered an hour later and resulted in that transfer being eliminated from the chain of blocks.

A year later, over 600 hundred users lost their Bitcoins when there was an information leak of passwords, electronic boxes and hashes at the *Mt Gox* stock exchange.

In June 2011, a user called *allinvain* claimed to have amassed 25,000 Bitcoins from mining before having his computer hacked and the Bitcoins stolen from his hard drive. We will leave you to do the maths on what the stolen Bitcoins would be worth today!

In an unregulated industry, there is no way to verify the credentials of a wallet service, particularly in a new and rapidly developing industry. In August 2011, one such wallet service called *My Bitcoin* disappeared from the Web. It was claimed at the time that the site had been hacked. Fraud or hacking, it mattered little to those that lost their Bitcoins.

Another online exchange, *Bitcoinia*, suffered a similar fate. This exchange operated on a shared hosting provider called *Linode*. *Bitcoinia* was hacked twice, first in March 2012 losing 46,703 Bitcoins and again in May 2012 when a further 18,000 Bitcoins were stolen.

In August 2012, the *Bitcoin Savings and Trust* was closed down by the regulators claiming it was a classic Ponzi scheme. The judge ordered the organiser, *Tendon Shavers*, to repay more than 40 million dollars to the victims who had lost 265,678 Bitcoins.

There have been other claims of Ponzi schemes the most notable being *OneCoin*. The *Italian Antitrust and Consumer Protection Authority* fined *OneCoin* 2.5 million euros for being a 'pyramid scheme'. The Swedish Government also launched an investigation but closed it without bringing any charges. There are cryptocurrencies launched with seemingly nefarious purposes, designed to make money for only one group of people: the cryptocurrency creators.

Another exchange called *Bitfloor* was hacked in September 2012 with the attackers stealing 24,000 Bitcoins.

The biggest hack occurred in February 2014 when it was reported 850,000 Bitcoins were stolen from customers of *Mt Gox*.

In January 2015 another 19,000 Bitcoins were hacked from the *Bitstamp* exchange. Another exchange, *Bitfinex* reported in August 2016 that 120,000 Bitcoins had been stolen. Worth approximately 77 million dollars, the company foisted these costs onto users forcing them to take a reduction in the value of their deposits equal to about 36 per cent. Both Bitstamp and Bitfinex are still current exchanges. In regards to Bitfinex, there are questions about the company's credibility with the New York Times saying that Bitfinex is an 'opaque operation that provides no information on its website about where it is, or who operates the company'.

Maybe the most recent hacking is December 2017 when *NiceHash* confirmed the loss of 4,700 Bitcoins.

An Australian Bitcoin user by the name of *TradeFortress* claims to have had 4,100 Bitcoins, owned by others, stolen from his website. Despite the Bitcoin being worth over one million dollars, TradeFortress was unlikely to report it to the police because, at that stage, a thief of Bitcoins had never been investigated by either federal or state police. Cryptocurrency theft would be treated like any other theft by the police, and only if it was reported by the victim.

It isn't just the big players that are hacked. Unfortunately, there is little way of knowing how many individuals get hacked. Most hacking probably goes unreported because the police in many countries don't have the resources nor skills required to find the hackers.

There are many newcomers to the world of cryptocurrencies and most are unaware of the risks making them easy prey for hackers and cyber thieves. Computer hacks, phishing attacks and Ponzi cryptocurrency schemes are all common types of cryptocurrency theft.

Hackers also trawl social media looking for conversations regarding cryptocurrency and match it with the investor's phone number and email address. In what is known as phone-porting attack, they call up the phone provider and, posing as the investor, attempt to have the customer service representative transfer the phone number of the investor to a device that they control. Controlling the phone number, the hackers can now reset the password, giving them complete access to the investor's cryptocurrencies.

Around January 2018, *Facebook* banned all cryptocurrency advertising because it was being frequently associated with financial grifts and high profile scams.

There appears to be an ever-growing list of fake Bitcoins due to the fact that they are relatively easy to make and maintain. Initially, creators of these new cryptocurrencies took advantage of the Bitcoin name because it was easier and cheaper to promote in the competitive crypto market. Today, for the better informed customers, this branding is now likely to backfire as people regard these as cheap imitations. Examples of some of these imitators include *Bitcoin Dark, Bitcoin Plus, Bitcoin Red, Bitcoin Scrypt, Bitcoin Z* and *United Bitcoin*. If purchasing Bitcoin, investors should always check its code. Bitcoin's official code is BTC so, if another code is being used, it is not the real Bitcoin and only worth a fraction of the real Bitcoin.

If a customer has mistakenly purchased fake Bitcoin, they can sell or swap the fake for the real Bitcoin or real world money by using an online service such as *ShapeShift* or an online exchange. If it is Bitcoin Cash that has been purchased then the customer may also use a Bitcoin ATM to convert to either Bitcoin or withdraw cash. Any user needs to exercise caution when using or purchasing cryptocurrencies to make sure the correct wallets are used and not be a soft target for hackers.

Computer hackers like those behind the *Wannacry* ransomware attack which infected nearly 100 countries, or the *Petya* cyber-attack of the Cadbury chocolate factory in Tasmania, have demanded that the ransom be paid with Bitcoin.

How to avoid hacks and scams

The unfortunate truth regarding cryptocurrencies is that many of the newly released coins fail, sometimes due to the lack of community support, and at other times due to code base and developer issues.

We have already mentioned the hacking of exchanges but, for newly released offerings, a person considering purchasing any cryptocurrency should ensure that everything is traded publicly and not within a private system that is closed and centralised. So one should look for one that had wallet software available and offered an open-source codebase and decentralised architecture.

For any investment whether it is shares, property or cryptocurrencies, if it sounds too good to be true, it usually is.

It may be worth considering what happens with one's crypto-currencies in the event of death or permanent disability, disappearance, mental illness or dementia. Unless another designated person has the private key, the owner's crypto-currencies will be lost forever. In the case of death for example, the user needs to make the executor of the will aware of the existence of any cryptocurrencies; and perhaps make a different person aware of the location of the private key. This is important because, before not too long, theft of cryptocurrencies may be perpetrated by executors of wills unless the ownership of the cryptocurrency is well documented and the private key is kept secret until it needs to be revealed.

13   Taxation

Since Bitcoin (beta version) first appeared in 2009, the popularity of Bitcoin, and now other cryptocurrencies, in recent years has forced Governments around the world to take note. The *Australian Taxation Office (ATO)* like many other government agencies is playing catch-up but is gaining ground.

Cryptocurrencies are subject to tax in Australia and the ATO will enforce the collection of the correct amount of tax to be paid. As the old saying goes, there are only two certainties – death and taxes; and cryptocurrencies has not changed the latter.

The ATO website states that "Bitcoin is neither money nor a foreign currency…Bitcoin is, however, an asset for Capital Gains Tax (CGT) purposes." When reference is made to Bitcoin, it also applies to other crypto or digital currencies that have similar characteristics to Bitcoin. It is fair to say that the ATO's view of cryptocurrencies is evolving. Some recent examples are:

From 1 July 2017, the sale and purchase of digital currencies like Bitcoin will no longer be subject to the Goods and Services Tax (GST). The amendments to the *GST Act and Regulations* were necessary to avoid double taxation. Prior to the amendments, consumers were being charged GST on the purchase of the digital currency and then paying GST on goods and services that were subject to GST when they made purchases using the digital currency.

Money laundering using cryptocurrencies has been touted as a major concern for Governments across the world. The ATO has assembled a task force to 'follow the money', investigate cryptocurrency transactions and ensure that these transactions appear on tax returns at the end of the financial year. They are also being assisted by the *Black Economy Taskforce*, credited with identifying an estimated 30 billion dollars in tax evasion through focusing on money laundering.

There have been a number of rulings and several income tax determinations relating to the application of tax laws in regard to Bitcoin and other digital currencies. Examples include:

- TD2014/26 Income Tax: is Bitcoin a CGT asset for the purpose of section 108-5(1) of the Income Tax Assessment Act 1997?
- TD2014/27 Income Tax: is Bitcoin trading stock for the purposes of subsection 70-10(1) of the Income Tax Assessment Act 1997?
- TD 2014/28 Fringe Benefits Tax: is the provision of Bitcoin by an employer to an employee in respect of their employment a property fringe benefit for the purposes of subsection 136(1) of the Fringe Benefits Tax Assessment Act 1986?

As with any venture that is subject to Australian taxation laws, there are some basic requirements that need to be followed to stay within the law.

There needs to be record keeping. Records need to be kept of all cryptocurrency transactions and must include the date of the transaction, what the transaction was for, the value in Australian dollars and details of the other party to the transaction; or, as a minimum, the cryptocurrency address. The amount in Australian dollars would need to be taken from a reputable online exchange to provide the verification necessary as to the exchange rate.

We do need to look at the various uses for cryptocurrency as these are treated differently for taxation purposes. If you have purchased a cryptocurrency to pay for personal goods and services acquired, for example, on the internet, there will be no income tax nor GST implications. If the cost of the cryptocurrency is $10,000 or less then any capital gain or loss from the disposal is disregarded for Capital Gains Tax. In contrast to this use for personal consumption, there is the purchase of cryptocurrency for speculative gain, whether you are a serious investor or not.

The best way to illustrate the tax treatment is by way of illustration:

Michelle is an accountant with a strong background in technology. In 2014, she decided that Bitcoin was the way of the future and purchased $3,000 worth of Bitcoin that she was going to use for the purchase of clothes and other personal items. However, the number of shops was limited at that time so no purchases were made but the value of her Bitcoin increased to $23,000 over the next couple of years. By 2017, the number of retailers accepting Bitcoin and the introduction of Bitcoin withdrawal machines meant that Michelle was able to purchase everything from a cup of coffee to clothing using her Bitcoin.

While Michelle's Bitcoin has had a capital gain of $20,000, she will pay no tax on that gain because her original purchase was under $10,000 and the Bitcoin was used to purchase items for personal consumption. If Michelle had originally purchased $13,000 of Bitcoin, the gain of $10,000 would be subject to CGT. The same rules for CGT apply to gains made on Bitcoin or any other cryptocurrency. As Michelle has held the Bitcoin for more than 12 months, she would be entitled to a 50% capital gains discount resulting in $5,000 being added to her taxable income for that year and being taxed at her marginal tax rate. The capital gain of $5,000 may be reduced further by any cost associated with acquiring or holding the Bitcoin.

The purchase by Michelle of goods such as a cup of coffee and clothing is regarded by the ATO as similar to a barter arrangement with similar tax consequences. Michelle would need to keep the following records for her Bitcoin transaction: the date of the transaction, the amount in Australian dollars, and details of the transaction and the other party.

Michelle had mentioned to her friend Brad how her Bitcoin had increased. Brad, a gambler by nature, decided that he would buy $1,000 worth of Bitcoin. When it increased in value in just over a week, Brad purchased another $1,000. Over a six-month period, Brad purchased $8,000 worth of Bitcoin which increased in value to $20,000. Brad decided to sell, fearing the bubble may burst. Despite his total purchases being less than $10,000, Brad will be subject to tax on his $12,000 profit. The $12,000 will be added to his taxable income and taxed at his marginal rate. There is no 50% exemption. Brad's intention at the time of purchase had been to make a profit on his purchases.

There is quite a large percentage of the population that, for one reason or another, doesn't have a will. Although dying intestate does create problems, there are normally physical assets like property, shares, bank accounts and cash that can be identified as part of the estate. This is not the case with an intangible 'asset' like cryptocurrencies. Heirs or executors need to know of any cryptocurrencies held, not only so that the cryptocurrencies aren't lost forever but also so that any tax may be calculated correctly for the beneficiaries.

If shares are inherited, CGT is not paid at that time but only when sold later. It is assumed that the ATO will treat cryptocurrencies in a similar way to shares. In order to determine any future CGT liability, it is important to keep sufficient records of the transactions for cryptocurrencies.

Apart from cryptocurrency being used for personal transactions and investment, it may also be used for business transactions. A business may receive cryptocurrency in full or part-exchange for supplying goods and services to a customer. In turn, it may pay for goods and services it receives in cryptocurrency. If the supply of the goods and services was a taxable supply, and the business is registered for GST, then the business may charge GST and claim input tax credits on the GST charged. The transactions will be treated as receiving non-cash consideration under the barter system and there are clear guidelines established by the ATO in this regard. To determine the value of the cryptocurrency in Australian dollars, the business would need to obtain a fair market value from a reputable cryptocurrency exchange. A business may also have to consider any capital gains consequences if more than $10,000 is disposed of.

14 Superannuation

Please note that this chapter is for educational purposes only and is not intended as investment advice. Before considering any cryptocurrency as an investment in superannuation, speak to your accountant for professional advice.

"Bitcoin is far too adventurous as an SMSF investment", "whether Bitcoin would exist in five years" or "Bitcoin is young technology with possible great potential but it experiences enormous volatility and its future is anything but certain" are some of the comments that have been made by professionals in the past.

Over the last year or two, the question has been asked as to whether cryptocurrency can be used to contribute to a superannuation fund or as an investment within a superannuation fund. As cryptocurrencies are still in their infancy, it is unlikely that any company will make superannuation contributions on behalf of their employees in cryptocurrencies for the foreseeable future.

At the date of publication of this book, there is no known industry or retail superannuation fund that will accept contributions to the fund in cryptocurrency or holds cryptocurrency as an investment. The only possible way of using cryptocurrency for contributions as well as an investment is through a Self-Managed Ssuperannuation Fund (SMSF). SMSF allows direct control over investment for retirement provided the sole purpose test is met and whether the investment strategy of the SMSF is satisfied. A person may want to consider cryptocurrency as an alternative investment to some of the traditional types of collectables such as coins, banknotes, art work or gold that may be used to diversify an investment portfolio within a SMSF. Like these other collectibles, cryptocurrencies do not pay any interest or dividend and rely solely on capital gains.

Before proceeding further, let us recap on a couple of the basics of a superannuation fund:

Superannuation is a vehicle used to accumulate wealth for a person's retirement. The main test against which any breach of superannuation is assessed is known as the sole purpose test and the sole purpose of superannuation is to provide for retirement benefits for members of the SMSF.

Each SMSF must have an investment strategy and the trust deeds of the SMSF must allow the investments listed in the investment strategy.

Any transactions in the superannuation fund should be at arm's length or in other words members of the fund or any related parties to the members are not allowed to deal with the superannuation fund. A common example to illustrate the sole purpose and arm's length transaction relates to the use of a holiday home or apartment owned by the superannuation fund. No members of the superannuation fund or any related parties whether direct or indirect family members or work related associates can use the home or apartment for accommodation as this would be deemed a benefit being gained and therefore not the sole purpose of providing for a person's retirement. Similarly, if the property was to be let through a real estate agency then no member of the real estate agency should be related to members of the superannuation fund.

As at the date of publishing this book, the Australian Taxation Office has not provided any formal ruling or publication on investing in cryptocurrencies like Bitcoin in a SMSF.

Before purchasing or transferring cryptocurrency to a self-managed superannuation fund, there are a few requirements that need to be satisfied:

1. Examine the trust deed of the SMSF to ensure that it will allow the purchase of cryptocurrency. If uncertain, ask an accountant to confirm that the trust deed allows this or to arrange to have the trust deed amended to allow the purchase of cryptocurrency as an investment.

2. If the trust deed allows cryptocurrency as an investment then examine the investment strategy of the fund to ensure that the investment strategy makes provision for cryptocurrency as an investment.

3. Agree upon the percentage range that will be permissible for the SMSF. The amount of cryptocurrency that may form part of the investment strategy will vary from person to person and needs to take into account the person's age, their attitude to risk, diversification, liquidity, the amount being considered for investment and the total amount in the fund. Also consider the other assets already held in the fund and whether adding cryptocurrency will add to the risk of the overall portfolio. This is particularly important if there are any derivatives in the SMSF. Remember, trustees for a SMSF are responsible for deciding what prudent investment decisions are. Cryptocurrency is a relatively new investment with potential high returns, but also high risk. This volatility needs to be weighed up in making the investment decision.

4. Approaching retirement age, an investment in any cryptocurrency may not be regarded as prudent as the risk of significant capital losses are high and it is not a stable income generating asset.

5. In pension phase, the value of any cryptocurrency will likely need to be valued at the end of each financial year so that the value of the pension to be withdrawn can be calculated. It is also important in pension phase that the trustees have sufficient funds available to pay the required pension.

6. Trustees in their thirty or forties looking to invest only a small percentage of the fund's assets in cryptocurrency may be able to argue that between 1 per cent and 5 per cent of the fund's assets in cryptocurrency does

not constitute a material risk for the fund, that the trustee has a number of years to recoup any losses before considering retirement and that cryptocurrencies do have the potential to increase the fund's overall investment performance.

7. The trustees need to be satisfied that any investment in cryptocurrency meets the needs and objectives of the SMSF and the investment strategy.

8. Not being a listed security or a commercial property, any cryptocurrency must be purchased from an unrelated party, for example an exchange. A SMSF cannot buy cryptocurrency from its members or associated parties.

9. As with bank accounts of the superannuation fund, extreme care needs to be exercised to ensure that private and superannuation funds are not mixed up. If any cryptocurrency is bought or sold, the funds for the purchase and from the sale need to come from, and be banked into, the superannuation fund bank account.

10. For simplicity and transparency, it is suggested that buying cryptocurrency direct is the prudent way to acquire any cryptocurrency and to avoid any purchases or dealings through multi-level marketing organisations where the sole-purpose test and related parties could be questioned.

11. The SMSF investments have to be clearly identified as being owned by the SMSF and this may prove difficult due to the secrecy and security surrounding cryptocurrencies.

12. Arrange a meeting with the SMSF auditor and explain the trustee's knowledge of the currency, how the cryptocurrency will be purchased, how it will be held and confirm with the auditor what information they will need to undertake the audit successfully. The auditor will need to sight evidence to verify the SMSF holdings

and all purchase and sales of the cryptocurrency. The auditor will want to be able to trace all transactions to identify trades, the value of those trades, the time and date when those trades occurred and who has authority to transact on the cryptocurrencies account. The auditor will also likely want to see that the cryptocurrency is securely stored and whether insurance has been considered.

In summary, does cryptocurrency;

- align with the investment plan?
- fit the risk versus reward profile?
- match the criteria for a long term sustainable investment?

Because cryptocurrencies are new, it is important to seek the advice of an accountant and the auditor who will be preparing the SMSF audit and tax return. Not all auditors will be comfortable in auditing a SMSF with investments in cryptocurrency. Being unfamiliar with this type of investment, the auditor may set the bar high in terms of checking the cryptocurrency activities which in turn is likely to increase the audit fees for the fund.

Understand that there are certain assets that can be acquired from related parties by 'in specie' contributions. The limited list of assets for 'in specie' contributions include business real property and listed shares and securities. Cryptocurrencies are currently not classified as an asset that can be acquired through 'in specie' contribution.

The person through whom the SMSF purchases the cryptocurrency should not be related in any way. Also, the trustees certainly should not sell to their superannuation fund any cryptocurrency owned by the trustees in their own name or a company name in which the trustees are directors or shareholders.

The Australian Taxation Office has decided that Bitcoin (cryptocurrencies) are not like 'foreign currency' in nature for the purpose of Division 775 of the Income Tax Assessment Act 1997. As a result, the SMSF will not be able to acquire cryptocurrencies from a member or related party of the SMSF. SMSFs should always purchase any cryptocurrencies through an exchange.

For tax purposes, any gains and losses in the SMSF as a result of cryptocurrency are taxed in exactly the same way as any other capital asset in the fund. That is, CGT may apply to any gains made on the sale or exchange of the cryptocurrency. If the cryptocurrency has been held for more than 12 months by the SMSF then the SMSF should qualify for the CGT discount of 33.33% for SMSFs. The concessional CGT rate is 10% or 0% if the SMSF is in retirement phase.

A breach of the *Superannuation Industry (Supervision) Act* and regulations commonly referred to as the SIS Act can result in the SMSF becoming non-complying. A non-complying fund may be subject to severe penalties, loss of its concessional tax rate and the asset also being taxed.

Unlike money held in a bank account which will earn some interest, cryptocurrencies do not earn any interest. They are more like some collectibles like rare coins or precious metals like gold that appreciate in value. However, unlike these coins or precious metals, cryptocurrencies are far more volatile and, for most people, the reason behind the demand, and therefore the volatility, is not understood. For many centuries, gold has been an acceptable form of payment for goods and services and then as a hedge against economic woes. It is unlikely that cryptocurrencies will provide the same functions as gold.

Undoubtedly, cryptocurrencies will make some people serious money but also people, potentially those same people, will lose serious money. People who tend to make their money in these types of speculative markets are ones that get in early, have a plan to make money at or near the top of the market, and then take their profits and get out. Like any market, whether it be the share market or the property market, nobody knows where the peak of the market is likely to be. The property market may be a little less forgiving in terms of time but the share market and cryptocurrencies can change very quickly.

One part of superannuation that is often overlooked is what happens with a superannuation in the event of a person's death. Superannuation is not covered by a will and it is at the discretion of the trustees as to how the superannuation balance is distributed. It is recommended that a Binding Death Benefit Nomination be in place which the trustees will follow.

The potential problems for the trustees of a superannuation fund, if the fund has any cryptocurrency as an asset, is firstly to be aware of the existence of the cryptocurrency and secondly how to access these digital assets. The challenge here is how to securely pass on details of the cryptocurrency holdings including the public and private keys without creating a security nightmare. Whoever has access to the public and private keys has access to the vault so they need to be very trustworthy otherwise the cryptocurrency could disappear without a trace.

15. How Other Countries View Cryptocurrencies

Countries across the world have, in general, been slow to react to cryptocurrencies and many reacted negatively initially. Cryptocurrencies do provide a threat to countries' sovereignty in two main areas: currency and taxation.

 Some countries still regard cryptocurrencies as illegal and impose fines and imprisonment for users, exchanges and miners.

Many other countries are now introducing legislation and rules regarding taxation associated with cryptocurrencies.

Germany was the first country to recognise Bitcoin as real currency. However, in January 2018, the finance ministers of both Germany and France agreed to launch a joint crackdown on the cryptocurrency markets, making a joint proposal to regulate the cryptocurrency at the next summit of the G20 group. The European Union has previously proposed treating cryptocurrency markets as a security threat due to activities such as money laundering and terrorism.

Germany's Central Bank director, Joachim Wuermeling, said that borderless cryptocurrencies are difficult to regulate within specific regions or countries and believes that they should be regulated through an international set of rules rather than national ones.

It is not just France and Germany calling for action. Russia is proposing a multinational cryptocurrency for BRICS and EEU which could potentially be used by more than 40 per cent of the world's population. So there are moves afoot by the world's super powers but will any agreement be reached?

It has been rumoured that South Korea was planning to shutdown cryptocurrency trading exchanges but these rumours may be incorrect. However, South Korea has new regulations to slow down speculative investing in cryptocurrencies by forcing banks to comply with new 'kyc – know your customer' rules and imposing fines on investors who refuse to cease using anonymity in using cryptocurrencies.

In December 2017, the Governor of the Bank of Japan, Haruhiko Kuroda, remarked; 'if it's a question of whether it's functioning like currencies as a form of payment or means of settlement, I don't think it is. [Bitcoin] is being traded for investing or for speculation'.

Japan's *SBI* banking group has invested in *CoolBitX*, a Taiwan based cryptocurrency hardware wallet developer. *CoolWallet* is a hardware device used to store private keys and interfaces with both iOS and Android devices via Bluetooth. SBI is said to be planning to issue its own cryptocurrency, directly tradeable with the Japanese yen allowing payments and instant P2P transfers. In conjunction with *Ripple*, SBI has co-launched *SBI Ripple Asia* aimed at banks in a number of ASEAN countries.

Since 2013, the Reserve Bank of India has opposed cryptocurrencies on the basis that it is a security risk for its citizens investing in decentralised currencies without an asset base. India has not banned nor made it illegal to hold cryptocurrencies and expects capital gains from the sale of cryptocurrencies to be declared for income tax purposes. A past Economic Affairs Secretary, Sharktikanta Das, has called for a ban on cryptocurrencies rather than try to regulate it. This is in contrast to the Finance Minister, Arun Jaitley's, speech in the 2018-19 Union Budget; 'The government does not consider cryptocurrencies legal tender or coin and will take all measures to eliminate use of these crypto-assets in financing illegitimate activities or as part of the payment system'. In regards to blockchain, Mr Jaitley said 'distributed ledger system or blockchain technology allows the organisation of any chain of records or transactions, without the need of intermediaries. The government will explore use of blockchain technology proactively for ushering in digital economy'.

A collective of about six of India's bigger exchanges has established a *Blockchain and Cryptocurrency Committee of India* to provide a voice for cryptocurrencies. There have also been calls for India to establish its own cryptocurrency but India appears to be taking a cautious approach to this suggestion.

In the USA, a federal judge in Texas declared Bitcoin a legal form of currency. Some states like Illinois, Arizona and Georgia are looking to allow Bitcoin as a payment for state taxes. It has also been suggested that consideration needs to be given to whether this could qualify as a tax event; that is, if one had purchased Bitcoin and it had increased in value by the time taxes were paid, the capital gain would be taxed. Illinois has established the *Blockchain and Distributed Ledger Task Force* which has published a report to the General Assembly looking at ways government can use blockchain as a 'cheaper and safer way to administer government'.

The price index for conversions from Bitcoin to US dollars, euros or pound sterling can be found through various exchanges.

While it appears that there are some differences of opinion in Russia on cryptocurrency, the Russian president Vladimir Putin has emphasised the importance of blockchain in the country and has set 1 July 2018 for finalisation of legislation on cryptocurrency. The central bank is not keen on retail traders and investors participating in cryptocurrency trading and there may be governance rules established around mining requiring legally recognised entities to conduct mining activities.

Not every country is embracing cryptocurrencies and some are actively making them illegal with penalties ranging from fines to imprisonment. Some of the countries may not surprise while others will. Like most issues related to cryptocurrency, the laws in various countries are being frequently updated.

At the time of writing, the following countries have made crypto-currencies illegal –

In September 2017, China banned the trading of Bitcoin and other cryptocurrencies. Individuals appear to continue to trade in cryptocurrencies through in-person trades and chat apps like *WeChat* and *Telegram*. Professional cryptocurrency trading companies are targeted by the Chinese Government.

Zhang Ye, director of the *China Securities Regulatory Commission Information Centre*, while acknowledging some blockchain applications may require decentralisation, believes they should be limited and most should be centralised. China is grappling with how to gain the benefits from blockchain while retaining complete control in a centralised system.

China has a history of taking technology for overseas, banning it and replacing the overseas product with a local but highly-regulated alternative. This has already happened in China with *Google, Facebook* and *Twitter* to name a few. China is likely to get cryptocurrency but it will be a Chinese-based and controlled digital currency.

Several arrests have been reported of Bitcoin traders in Nepal since 2017.

Cryptocurrencies have never been legalised in Bolivia and again there have been reports of fines and arrests for repeat offenders for trading and mining of cryptocurrencies.

In mid-2014, Ecuador outlawed cryptocurrencies as part of its financial reform plans. Ecuador has its own digital currency system, not based on any blockchain technology, so the ban is likely to be a way of reducing competition.

The Morocco government officially outlawed cryptocurrency transactions in November 2017.

In Egypt, the foremost religious leader has called for a blockchain ban, stating that Bitcoin was illegal under *Sharia Law*. At the same time, it is reported that Egyptian authorities are mining cryptocurrency using citizen's computers and laptops. There are reports of a similar occurrence in Turkey.

While blockchain is generally accepted as a new and valuable technology, it is Bitcoin and the other cryptocurrencies that some countries appear to have problems with and governments are taking stances. From what has been seen to date, governments will only support blockchain and cryptocurrencies if they have introduced, or will introduce, legislation and regulations.

16. How Are Banks Reacting?

It would be easy to expect the banks to react badly to the attack by cryptocurrency on what has been their domain for centuries. But the reaction from banks seem to be mixed. There are reports of banks delaying transfer of funds used to purchase cryptocurrencies, leading to frustration on the part of the customers. On the other hand, there are reports of purchases through credit cards being prohibited by major banks around the world. Some banks have had these bans in place since 2015 but the market volatility around December 2017 and January 2018 saw other banks implementing bans in order to protect customers. The banks feared customers making risky purchasers on their credit cards or scammers purchasing cryptocurrencies and vanishing.

Banking regulators around the world are concerned about money laundering and require banks to monitor their customer accounts. This becomes increasingly difficult if the local currency is converted into cryptocurrency.

Some American banks such as *JP Morgan Chase, Citigroup* and *Bank of America* have stopped their customers from using their credit cards to buy cryptocurrencies due to fears that the volatility of the currencies will lead to customers being unable to repay their credit card debts.

Similar action has been taken by some of the largest banks in the United Kingdom with *Lloyds Bank, Virgin Money* and *Capital One* banning the use of credit cards to purchase cryptocurrencies and most other major banks monitoring the situation carefully.

17   A Bubble

What is a bubble?

We have seen the headlines such as Sydney Housing Bubble, Property Bubble to End, Bitcoin Bubble to Burst and many others but what is a bubble?

In a financial context, where the price for an asset exceeds its fundamental value by a large margin, this is normally referred to as a bubble.

In an article written by *John Lindeman*, a respected property market analyst in Australia, he compared a boom and a bubble as 'while booms may be founded on genuine demand, bubbles are fuelled by speculative buying frenzies which have nothing to do with the underlying utility value of the asset being purchased. They only last while more and more investors are lured in by the apparent certainty of massive financial gains and they can end without warning'.

Hyman Minsky, an economist, suggested five stages of a bubble and, in terms of Bitcoin, we can identify four of the five stages – The first stage is where investors get enamoured by such things as new technology or historically low interest rates and this is called the displacement stage. Stage two, or boom stage, has prices rising slowly then, as more investors enter the market and the asset receives more media attention, the prices start to rise rapidly as more investors enter through fear of missing out on this once-in-a-lifetime opportunity. Stage three sees caution thrown to the wind and prices skyrocket. During this euphoric stage, investors try to justify the rapid and relentless price rises and suggest new valuation methods and metrics. Stage four is where profit-taking occurs and may reflect the sell-off of Bitcoin in December 2017. Smart investors, particularly those that may have purchased at the start of the boom, start selling out. In the fifth stage, panic sets in as investors and speculators try to liquidate their investments at any price causing the price to plunge.

Bitcoin is starting to mature and may have moved past being a fad and may become a potential future currency and an investment.

One of the difficulties with Bitcoin and other cryptocurrencies as an investment is quantifying the underlying value of Bitcoin or any of the other cryptocurrencies. Unlike money in a bank, it doesn't earn any interest, it doesn't pay dividends from profits of a company like shares do, and nor does it earn rent like property.

As a currency, it is not aligned to a national economy like any of the fiat currencies. (Read our book "It's My Time: The A to Z of Property and Financial Terms" for further details on fiat currency). So how do you value Bitcoin and in turn be able to recognise when the price is diverging from its fundamentals and possible becoming a bubble?

So what may the fundamentals of Bitcoin and other cryptocurrencies be if there is no interest, dividends, rent or alignment to a national currency? This is unchartered waters in that there has never before been a Bitcoin.

There have been a few suggestions to attribute fundamentals to Bitcoin and other cryptocurrencies, none of which align with basic fundamentals of other assets such as shares, property or currencies.

Firstly, it is suggested that the supply of Bitcoins in the market is one fundamental. The technology behind Bitcoin itself regulates the supply; only 21million can be produced. The cost of producing Bitcoin (for example electricity and hardware requirements) and the reduction in the number that can be produced is making it less profitable to mine Bitcoin and may reach the stage where it is no longer economical to mine Bitcoin at all.

Secondly, it is suggested <u>that the value of a cryptocurrency</u> be based on the number of cryptocurrency transactions in a market through purchase of goods or services or any commodity. This again may be difficult to quantify because Bitcoin is not being used just to purchase goods and services but is being stored in the hope of future price increases. In 2016, Bitcoin's share of the total global cryptocurrency market was around 91.3 per cent but since then it has been losing market share to other cryptocurrencies like *Litecoin* and *Ethereum* and Bitcoin's share is now estimated at around 59.4 per cent.

Another proposed fundamental is based on the energy consumed by Bitcoin miners. However, other cryptocurrencies like Litecoin are more efficient and use less energy while others have more functionality like Ethereum's ability to execute smart contracts.

Bitcoin and the other cryptocurrencies may develop some fundamentals if larger investors like banks and hedge funds enter the market. Secondly, government regulation, which will be inevitable, may provide some stability and reduce the volatility.

Some people have been calling Bitcoin a bubble even back in 2013 when Bitcoin was around US$35. Is it just the fear of missing out (FOMO) that is driving up the price of Bitcoin and creating a potential bubble. Other cryptocurrencies like *Ripple* have also been called a bubble.

Another major concern is the number of other cryptocurrencies in the market place, many of which are not currencies but are commodities, energy or businesses.

If we look at history, the *1636 Dutch Tulip Mania, the 1720 South Seas Company Bubble, 1929 Wall Street Crash, 1999 DotCom Bubble* and even more recently in Australia with the mining property crashes in Queensland and Western Australia, there are some similarities. Graphs produced by John Lindeman of the *Wall Street Stock Market Crash 1929* and the *Moranbah House*

Price Crash 2013-17 show the similarities with the Bitcoin Crash in December 2017 and January 2018.

The Dutch Tulip Mania of the 1630s is still regarded as the benchmark by which bubbles are measured. Over a number of years the popularity for the tulips grew but supply was limited due to their growing time. Prices grew and grew until, in 1636, the prices peaked and then started to collapse from February 1637. Within a matter of a few months, tulip prices were one-hundredth of what they were at their peak. History is littered with such bubbles which Minsky argues are inevitable in a free-market economy.

Bloomberg's Stephen Gandel has estimated, based on valuation, that Bitcoins are four times more expensive than dot.com stocks at the height of the dot.com bubble. A senior lecturer in finance at the *University of Technology in Sydney, Adrian Lee,* does not believe that a Bitcoin bubble would pose a risk to the global economy because there is not as much money tied up as there was during the dot.com bubble. Mr Lee thought that the people most likely to suffer in a Bitcoin crash were the speculators, people who use Bitcoin, those with mining infrastructure, ICO-based businesses and maybe the exchanges.

Dr Jason Potts, Professor of Economics at RMIT Melbourne thinks the chances of a systematic crash are extremely low, pointing out that there have been some big crashes, crashes of up to 80 per cent, and the economy has recovered. There is an enormous amount of volatility but there is also a long-term growth trend in Bitcoin in particular.

The impact on other cryptocurrencies would depend on what sparked the crash. A crack-down by the central banks around the world on Bitcoin is likely to result in other cryptocurrencies also falling. If the crash was as a result of irrational exuberance, like we have seen, then it is likely that only those cryptocurrencies that have seen a sharp rise are likely to see dramatic drops.

People most likely to be affected are those who have bought at the wrong time, and at a high price, while others that have been waiting on a crash are most likely to be happy buying the cryptocurrency at a reasonable price.

Bitcoin may not be in a bubble but it certainly has had some of the stages that Minsky identified. We have seen a lot of price volatility over Bitcoin's short history and this is likely to continue.

18   Closing Thoughts

Blockchain, cryptocurrencies and the future

Will cryptocurrencies sound the death knell of traditional financial services including central banks? We can't tell. Yes, it appears that Bitcoin in particular has defied its detractors but unfortunately there is also a plethora of other cryptocurrencies that have failed.

No one knows what Bitcoin or any of the cryptocurrencies will be worth in the future. We know that Bitcoin has a limited supply of 21 million coins and that each is divisible by 8 decimal places. Does this provide sufficient scarcity to drive up prices or keep prices high? Does it provide the scarcity or security for Bitcoin to become a 'safe haven' as gold or the replacement for gold during times of economic trouble?

Prior to Christmas 2017, the price of Bitcoin was reaching lofty heights but then took a dramatic fall, falling from a high of $19,796 per Bitcoin on 17 December plummeting five days later to $11,590, according to data from *Coinbase*. The fall continued in 2018 and other coins like *Ethereum* also joined the fall in value. We see spectacular booms but also the spectacular busts. No doubt it will rise again and probably go even higher but will people accept a commodity with such sharp fluctuations as a safe haven in place of a tried and tested commodity like gold?

Facebook has removed posts relating to Bitcoin and crypto-currencies due to fraudulent activities and some major banks have stopped purchases of Bitcoin and other cryptocurrencies via credit cards due to the current dramatic price fluctuations. The one certainty is that nobody knows what Bitcoin or any of the other cryptocurrencies will be worth in the future.

The legitimacy of cryptocurrencies has been enhanced by the prospect of being listed on some major stock exchanges. With a number of countries like China openly opposing cryptocurrencies, it would appear that the likelihood of a global digital cash society is some years away. Australian banks are introducing new technology to allow instantaneous payments. This would certainly negate one of the cryptocurrencies' big selling points. It is hard to believe that the Australian banks would have introduced this change if it had not been for cryptocurrencies. We cannot foretell what is likely to happen with any of the cryptocurrencies. They may or may not be suitable for an investment in a person's SMSF and we have looked at the various issues to consider in this regard.

Bitcoin is popular due to its anonymous transactions and lack of fees. The transactions are irreversible and Bitcoin is subject to wild fluctuations in price. The anonymous nature of Bitcoin also makes it popular for illegal dealings. Bitcoins in the early days were used by drug cartels and arms dealers to launder their money and trade between each other to avoid the authorities and regulatory bodies. Bitcoin was used in the *Silk Road* that allowed the user to purchase pretty much everything available via the Silk Road anonymously.

At an investor conference, the boss of *JP Morgan* is reported as saying that if any of his staff were caught trading Bitcoin, he would fire them in a second and further described cryptocurrency as a fraud. This might now be considered an extreme view although not isolated. *Warren Buffett* has also said that he wouldn't be buying Bitcoin but that is in line with his philosophy that he must understand the business that he buys into.

There is a sudden shift in paradigm in terms of technology and jargon used in the blockchain and cryptocurrency applications. We have detailed all the major acronyms used in the blockchain and cryptocurrency in the following section. The general audience or bank customer is used to bank accounts, transaction of funds, and a name attached to the bank account. The general public is a little confused with terms like digital wallet, hot storage, cold storage, mining, anonymous transaction, dry code in smart contracts, wet code like law, legislations and so on.

The concept of cryptocurrency (like Bitcoin) may succeed in countries where there was a huge amount of financial damage caused by hyperinflation. In the case of Bitcoin, 50 Bitcoins were given out every ten minutes for four years (2009 to 2012), 25 Bitcoins were given out every 10 minutes for four years (2012 to 2016) and so on. There will no more Bitcoins after 2140.

The form of money in the past 10,000 plus years has been transforming from physical to digital. The mining of cryptocurrency is not by tunnelling into the earth but by using computers to solve complex mathematical problems.

The central banks are printing currency with no prescribed limits hence creating an additional burden on the society: inflation. Each piece of cryptocurrency is backed by cryptography and mathematics in the same way that each dollar is being backed by the governments. A fiat currency (printed note) average life span is around 27 years.

There are still likely to be major changes in cryptocurrencies. Cryptocurrencies are designed to be decentralised, possess a distributed ledger system and be self-regulated. Pseudonyms are used to protect the privacy of coin holders. Governments may have sat on the sidelines to see what would happen with the likes of Bitcoin and other cryptocurrencies but now Governments around the world are creating regulations around cryptocurrencies. Banks and other institutions are working together to counter some of the claims of cryptocurrencies in terms of speed of access and fees. But banks also seem to be acting responsibly to protect people purchasing cryptocurrencies in a rapidly rising market.

Governments across the world are paying attention to Bitcoin and the other cryptocurrencies and, in Australia, the ATO is closely watching developments. They have published guidelines and more is likely to be heard as the ATO looks to make sure that they are collecting the correct amount of tax from all taxpayers. Blockchain and some of the new variations, on the other hand, appears to have a very bright future with the distinct possibility of revolutionising many industries. A large number of diverse industries are trialling the blockchain technology.

There is a lot of information to become familiar with, and consequences to understand, in the emerging world of blockchain and cryptocurrencies. Already we have seen a number of cryptocurrencies emerge from the shadows of Bitcoin and many more crash and burn. Blockchain is likely to be superseded by updated versions, for example Hashgraph. What we have seen in the last few years may just be the tip of the iceberg. The growth of blockchain has led to a shortage of trained professionals and now universities like RMIT in Melbourne are starting to offer short courses in blockchain to meet the need.

As we said at the start of this book, the information in this book should not be interpreted as an endorsement of cryptocurrencies nor a recommendation to invest in any cryptocurrencies. As with other investments, historic performance is no guarantee of future returns. As an investment class, cryptocurrencies are very speculative investments and investing in cryptocurrencies involves significant risks – they are highly volatile, vulnerable to hacking and capital loss, and sensitive to secondary activity. Before investing you should obtain sound independent advice and decide whether the potential return outweighs the risks.

As with any investment, cryptocurrencies could be part of your investment strategy but, being a speculative investment, it should be a small percentage of your overall investment strategy. As a number of promoters point out, you should only invest that amount that you are prepared to lose. As with share and Forex investing, develop the discipline to take some of any profits along the way and use those to put into other proven long term asset classes.

As with any investment, if you are going to invest in any asset class then it pays to understand what you are doing. This is particularly true of any speculative investments. Avoid the herd mentality and make rational decisions on well-founded research.

Glossary of Terms

Blockchain and cryptocurrencies have developed their unique terminology such that we did not want to include those terms in our first book, *It's My Time: The A to Z of Property and Financial Terms.*

We have aimed to provide here as inclusive a glossary of terms as we could muster. As blockchain and cryptocurrency develop, we expect that terminology specific to these will also develop further.

51% attack is one of the ways to disrupt a cryptocurrency's blockchain by controlling more than 51% of the network. This requires massive computing power and, while possible on paper, the resources, coordination and finances required to do this would make it almost impossible to achieve. In this case, a 51% attack is only theoretical.

A

Address is essentially the same as your email address and it can be shared publicly with those who wish to send and receive cryptocurrency. It is a string of alphanumeric characters that represent a destination or origin from where, and to which, cryptocurrencies are sent. All addresses are unique.

Airdrop was first attempted with *Auroracoin* in early 2014 and is a method of distributing cryptocurrency among a population.

Algorithm is a set of mathematical instructions or rules that need to be followed in problem solving.

Altcoin or Alternative coin is a collective name given to all other cryptocurrencies that are not Bitcoin. These include Ethereum, Golem, Monero, Ripple, Dash, Litecoin, Dogecoin and many others.

AML is an acronym for *Anti-Money Laundering* laws which are a series of regulations designed to prevent money being converted from criminal activity into what appear to be legitimate assets.

Angel Investor is a wealthy individual who provides startup businesses with capital in exchange for debt or equity in the business.

Arbitrage refers to taking advantage of a difference in price of the same commodity on two different exchanges. An example would be the prices of ETH on the Korean exchanges against the prices on US exchanges.

ASIC is the acronym for *Application Specific Integrated Circuit* which is a computer processing chip that is designed to perform one function and one function only. Most modern computers have multi-thread CPUs that allow the computer to complete a range of tasks all at the same time, whereas an ASIC computer focusses only on one function. It may also offer significant power savings. In the crypto-space, an ASIC computer is used to mine Bitcoin.

ASIC Miner is a computer that contains an ASIC chip that is used to mine for Bitcoins by executing one task at a much faster rate than any normal desktop or laptop might allow. Computers that only process SHA256 are used to mine new coins on the Bitcoin blockchain. There are also ASICs for *Scrypt* which specifically solves the mathematical code for cryptocurrency like *Litecoin*.

ATH is the acronym for *All Time High*.

Attack Surface refers to the number of areas that are vulnerable to malicious users gaining access to the system. Generally the more complex the software, the higher the attack surface.

B

Bagholder refers to someone still holding an altcoin after a pump-and-dump crash or holding a coin that is sinking in value with few future prospects.

Bearish is where there is an expectation that price is going to decrease.

Bear Trap is a manipulation of a stock or commodity by investors. Traders who 'set' the bear trap do so by selling stock until it fools other investors into thinking its upward trend in value has stopped, or is dropping. Those who fall into the bear trap will often sell at that time, fearing a further drop in value. At that point, those who set the trap will buy at the low price and will release the trap – which is essentially a false bear market. Once the bear trap is released, the value will even out, or even climb.

Bear market is a market where prices are going down (downtrend).

Bip is the acronym for *Bitcoin Improvement Proposals*. These are the proposed by the members of the Bitcoin community to improve features of Bitcoin.

Bit is a unit of information expressed as either a 0 or 1 in binary notation. In regard to Bitcoin, it is a common unit used to designate a sub-unit of a Bitcoin – 1,000,000 bits is equal to one Bitcoin. This unit is more convenient for pricing tips, goods and services.

Bitcoin is not controlled by a centralized government or agency. The Bitcoin network is designed to mathematically generate no more than 21 million Bitcoins and was designed to regulate itself to deal with inflation.

Bitcoin Network is the decentralised, peer-to-peer network which maintains the blockchain. This processes all Bitcoin transactions.

Bitcoin Protocol is the open-source, cryptographic protocol which operates on the Bitcoin network, setting the 'rules' for how the network runs.

Bitcoin (unit of currency) is 100,000,000 *satoshis*. A unit of the decentralised, digital currency which can be traded for goods and services. Bitcoin also functions as a reserve currency for the altcoin ecosystem.

BitcoinJS is an online library of *javascript* code used for Bitcoin development, particularly web wallets.

BitcoinQT is an open source software client used by PCs. It contains a copy of the blockchain and, once installed, it turns the PC into a node in the Bitcoin Network. It also acts as a 'desktop wallet'.

Bitcoin Days Destroyed is an estimate for the 'velocity of money' within the Bitcoin network. This is used because it gives greater weight to Bitcoins that have not been spent for a long time. It better represents the level of economic activity taking place with Bitcoin than 'total transaction volume per day'.

Blocks are digital files where data pertaining to a cryptocurrency network is permanently recorded. A block records some or all of the most recent transactions that have not yet entered any prior blocks. Thus a block is like a page of a ledger or record book. Each time a block is 'completed', it gives way to the next block in the blockchain. A block is thus a permanent store of records which, once written, cannot be altered or removed. With Bitcoin, transactions are typically updated every 10 minutes.

Blockchain is a series of linked databases which form the backbone of the Bitcoin network. It is a digital ledger in which transactions made in Bitcoin are recorded chronologically and publicly. It is the authoritative record of every Bitcoin transaction that has ever occurred.

Block Explorer is a search engine for a cryptocurrency. It allows queries on transactions, addresses and other information.

Block Height is the number of completed blocks in the blockchain preceding the genesis (first) block on the chain. A genesis block will always have a height of zero as nothing precedes it. It is a metric used to create a bearing on time in the programming world. If the block height on January 1, 2014, was approximately 280,000, then it means that there were 280,000 blocks stacked on top of the first block created in January 2009 (inception of Bitcoin, first Bitcoin mined).

Block Reward – The coins that are paid to the computer (or pool of computers) that finds a working hash or solves the mathematical equation to complete a block in the mining process of cryptocurrencies. The reward for mining a Bitcoin block is 12.5 Bitcoins per block mined and this will halve every 210,000 blocks.

Bollinger Bands use historical data in a market to indicate possible volatility.

BTC is a common unit term to designate one Bitcoin.

Bullish refers to an expectation that price is going to increase.

Bull Market is a market where prices are going up (uptrend).

C

Cold Storage is the process of moving crypto-currency 'offline' as a means of safekeeping it from hacking. The most common methods used include a paper wallet, which involves printing out the QR code of a software wallet and storing it somewhere safe, like a safety deposit box, or moving the files of a software wallet onto a USB drive, or using an offline computer storage. It is one of the most effective security techniques. The key is generated on an offline system (one never connected to the internet) and stored offline either on a paper or a memory stick.

Cold Wallet is a wallet used for cold storage by not being connected to the internet.

Coloured Coins is an amount of Bitcoin repurposed to express another asset. The term 'colour' refers to the idea of giving special meaning through an addition of an attribute; there are no colours in coloured coins. Note: Bitcoin is programmable money. There is a function to change the attributes of the Bitcoin.

Confirmation is where all transactions on the blockchain are verified by all nodes – each verification of the transaction is called a confirmation. Coinbase requires three confirmations to consider a Bitcoin transaction final.

Consensus is achieved when all participants of the network agree on the validity of the transactions, ensuring that databases are exact copies of each other.

Cosigner is an additional person or entity that has partial control over a wallet.

Crypto Currency or cryptocurrency, also known as tokens, is a digital or virtual currency that uses advanced cryptography for security. A cryptocurrency is difficult to counterfeit because of this security feature. It is not issued by any central authority, rendering it theoretically immune to government interference or manipulation.

Cryptographic Hash Function produces a fixed size and unique hash value from variable size transaction input. The SHA256 computational algorithm is an example of a cryptographic hash.

Cryptography is the process of using codes and ciphers to encrypt and decrypt sensitive information, messages or data. It is used to create and secure wallets, sign transactions and verify the blockchain by the use of mathematics.

D

Dapp is an acronym for a decentralized application that is open source, operates autonomously, has its data stored on a blockchain, incentivised in the form of cryptographic tokens and operates on a protocol that shows proof-of-value. This refers to an application that uses an *Ethereum* smart contract as its back-end code. *Dapps* are renowned for having proven 100% uptime.

DAO is an acronym for *Decentralised Autonomous Organizations* It is a 'blockchain technology inspired' organization or corporation that exists and operates without human intervention; an investor-directed venture capital fund built on the Ethereum network that was hacked in June 2016. The hack stole about a third of the DAO's funds and led to Ethereum being hard-forked the following month. The DAO is often cited as one of Ethereum's biggest stumbles thus far.

DDoS Attack is an attack on a server or network intended to suspend or interrupt the services it provides. DDOS is an acronym for *'Distributed Denial of Service-Attack'*. A DDoS is a cyberattack utilizing many different computers to tie up the resources of a website or web service. Some Bitcoin exchanges have come under DDoS attacks.

Darksend is *Darkcoin*'s decentralized mixing implementation, which was designed to give users of Darkcoin greater transactional privacy/anonymity.

Deep Web is where the content online is not indexed by search engines, making it difficult to access. The majority of content on the internet resides on the deep web and can be accessed using a program called *TOR*. This is also where illegal sites such as *Silk Road* exist.

Deflation is a decrease in the general price level of goods in an economy. Traditionally this has taken place when a currency's demand collapses; however it is a natural property of Bitcoin.

Demurrage is where certain currencies penalise users for hoarding by charging a fee for holding unspent coins. This fee increases as time passes.

Denomination

Bitcoin was designed to increase in value as time goes by. This is due to a limited number of Bitcoins (21 million). Bitcoin is mostly expressed in three major denominations.

1BTC = 1 full Bitcoin

1 milli Bitcoin = 1mBTC = 1 thousandth of a Bitcoin
1 micro Bitcoin = 1uBTC

Desktop Wallet is a wallet that stores the private keys on your computer, allowing the spending and management of Bitcoins.

Deterministic Wallet is a wallet based on a system of deriving multiple keys from a single starting point known as a seed. This seed is all that is needed to restore a wallet if it is lost and can allow the creation of public addresses without the knowledge of the private key.

Difficulty is a measure of the amount of computing power required to solve the hash of a block. This increases to counteract increasing network hash rate in order to maintain a 10 minute confirmation time. It re-adjusts every 2016 blocks.

Digital Signature is a digital code generated by public key encryption that is attached to an electronically transmitted document to verify its contents and the sender's identity.

Distributed and Central ledger are two ledgers. A distributed ledger is an agreement of shared, replicable and synchronized data, in this case spread across multiple networks, across many CPU's. A central ledger, is the opposite in that all of the data, while being synchronized and replicable, is controlled by a singular network or individual.

Double Spending is the act of spending the same Bitcoins twice. The blockchain plus Bitcoin mining exists to confirm all transactions and to prevent such fraud.

Dust Transactions are transactions so small that they are considered 'spam' by the network. They are not relayed in order to stop people accidentally or deliberately clogging the blockchain.

E

EEA is an acronym for *Enterprise Ethereum Alliance* which is a coalition of startups and corporations trying to figure out the best way to use Ethereum.

Elliptic Curve Cryptography is a type of asymmetric or public key cryptography based on the discrete logarithm. Bitcoin uses a specific elliptic curve and set of mathematical constants, as defined in the standard called secp256k1.

Escrow is the practice of having a third party act as an intermediary in a transaction. This third party holds the funds on and sends them off when the transaction is completed.

ETF is an acronym for *Exchange Traded Fund* which is an investment fund traded on stock markets that track the price index of an underlying asset.

EVM or Ethereum Virtual Machine is a Turing complete virtual machine that allows anyone to execute arbitrary EVM Byte Code. Every Ethereum node runs on the EVM to maintain consensus across the blockchain.

Ethereum is a blockchain-based decentralized platform for apps that run smart contracts and is aimed at solving issues associated with censorship, fraud and third party interference.

Exchange is a central platform for exchanging different forms of cryptocurrencies. Typically, Bitcoin exchanges are used to exchange cryptocurrency for traditional monetary units.

F

Faucet is a website which gives away free Bitcoins or other cryptocurrency to any IP address that connects to them.

Fees are included by the sender of a transaction to the network for processing the requested transaction. Most transactions require a minimum fee of 0.5mBTC (1 mBTC = 1 thousandth of a BTC).

FOMO is the acronym for *Fear of Missing Out* which is a mindset that causes people to purchase a stock or cryptocurrency based on the premise that they may miss out on a good thing.

Fork is a split resulting in a new (updated) version of the original cryptocurrency. A fork happens when there is a major update that requires a new version of software to be implemented. A fork is the permanent divergence of an alternative operating version of the current blockchain. Forks come into existence when a 51% attack occurs, a bug in the program, or more commonly a new set of consensus rules come into existence. These happen when a development team creates and inserts notably substantial changes into the system. The successful fork is decided by the height of their blocks.

Frictionless. In reference to payment systems, the system is 'frictionless' when there are zero transaction costs or restraints on trading.

Frontier, Homestead, Metropolis, Serenity are the four planned stages of the Ethereum development roadmap. We are currently in the Homestead phase. The Metropolis update is likely to be available shortly.

FUD is the acronym for *Fear, Uncertainty and Doubt* that result from rumours and misinformation that can have an effect on a stock or a crypto that causes people to sell their holdings. It is sometimes distributed deliberately to cause confusion and lend an advantage to those who start the spread of information.

FUDster is someone who is spreading FUD.

G

Gas is a measurement of how much processing is required by the Ethereum network to process a transaction. Simple transactions, like sending Ether to another address, typically do not require much gas. More complex transactions, like deploying a smart contract, require more gas.

Gas Price is the amount of Ether to be spent for each gas unit on a transaction. The initiator of a transaction chooses and pays the gas price of the transaction. Transactions with higher gas prices are prioritized by the network.

Genesis Block is the first block, or first few blocks, in the blockchain.

GPU is an acronym for *graphics processing unit* which is a specialised processor originally designed for the high graphics requirements of computer games. These are also used to mine cryptocurrency since they outperform CPUs.

Gwei is another denomination of Ether. Gas prices are most often measured in Gwei. 1 Ether = 1000000000 Gwei. (10^9)

H

Halving occurs where the 'reward' for successfully mining a block of Bitcoin is reduced by half. For Bitcoin, the reward is halved after 210,000 blocks are mined and then every 210,000 thereafter.

Hard Fork is a complete change to the protocol used for a particular cryptocurrency. It is a complete divergence from the previous software version of the blockchain for a cryptocurrency, and nodes running previous versions will no longer be accepted by the newest version.

Hardware Wallet is a device that can securely store cryptocurrency. Hardware wallets are often regarded as the most secure way to hold cryptocurrency.

Hodl is a meme resulting from someone on a Bitcoin forum who is posting while drunk and makes a post with this typo in place of 'hold'.

I

ICO is the acronym for *Initial Coin Offering* which is similar to an *Initial Public Offering* in the non-crypto world. Startups issue their own tokens for funding.

Inflation is an increase in the general price level of goods in an economy.

Inputs is in reference to an output of a previous transaction. Inputs to an address are added up and this amount determines the amount a wallet can spend in outputs.

J

JOMO is the acronym for *Joy of Missing Out*.

K

Kimoto Gravity Well is a 'mining difficulty readjustment' algorithm, which was created in 2013 for *Megacoin*, an altcoin. The well allows difficulty readjustment to occur every block, instead of every 2016 blocks for Bitcoin. This was done as a response to concern about multi-pool mining schemes.

KYC is the acronym for *Know Your Customer,* used to describe a series of laws and regulations which require businesses to know the identity of their customers.

L

Laundry is also known as a 'mixing service', combining funds from various users and redistributing them, making tracing the Bitcoins back to their original source very difficult by mixing their 'taint'.

Ledger is a physical or electronic log book containing a list of transactions and balances typically involving financial accounts. The Bitcoin blockchain is the first distributed, decentralized public ledger.

Leverage is often used to describe trading with borrowed capital (margin) in order to increase the potential return of an investment. It also increases potential losses.

Litecoin is one of the first notable 'altcoins'. It was created by *Bobby Lee* to be a 'silver to Bitcoin's gold'. Litecoin uses the *Scrypt* mining algorithm instead of SHA256, it has a 2.5 minute confirmation time, and has a total coin supply of 84 million coins.

Limited order / limited buy/ limited sell are orders placed by traders to buy or sell a cryptocurrency when the price meets a certain amount.

Liquidity is the availability of an asset to be bought and sold easily without affecting its market price.

Liquidity Swap is a financial instrument (contracts) on cryptocurrency exchanges where investors offer loans to others to trade with in exchange for a set return.

M

MACD or Moving Average Convergence Divergence, is a trend indicator that shows the relationship between two moving averages of prices.

Margin Trading is the trading of assets or securities bought with borrowed money. A trader usually contributes an initial amount which is then used as collateral for their debt.

Market Cap is the total value held in a cryptocurrency. It is calculated by multiplying the total supply of coins by the current price of an individual unit.

Market Order is a buy or sell order which is executed at whatever the market price is at the time.

Merged Mining allows a miner to work on multiple blockchains simultaneously, contributing to the hash rate (and thus security) of both currencies being mined. For example, *Namecoin* has implemented merged mining with Bitcoin.

Merkle Root is the hash of all the hashes of all transactions in the block. Every transaction has a hash associated with it.

Merkle Tree contains a summary of all the transactions in the block.

MEW is the acronym for *MyEtherWallet* which is a free site that can generate *Ethereum* software wallets.

Micro-transaction is a financial transaction involving tiny sums of money. Traditionally amounts under a dollar have been impractical due to transaction fees; however, cryptocurrencies have the potential to change this.

mBTC is a Bitcoin metric of one thousandth of a Bitcoin (0.001 BTC).

Miners are computer operators who add new transactions to blocks and verify blocks created by other miners in return for transaction fees and rewarded with new cryptocurrency for their services.

Mining is the process by which transactions are verified and added to the public ledger, known as the blockchain, and also the means through which new Bitcoins are released. Anyone with access to the internet and suitable hardware can participate in mining. The mining process involves compiling recent transactions into blocks and trying to solve a computationally-difficult puzzle or algorithm. The participant who first solves the puzzle gets to place the next block on the block chain and claim the rewards. The rewards, which incentivize mining, are both the transaction fees associated with the transactions compiled in the block as well as a newly-released Bitcoin. (*Source: Investopedia.com*).

Mining Algorithm is the algorithm used by a cryptocurrency to sign transactions; these vary across different cryptocurrencies. Bitcoin's mining algorithm is SHA256, whilst *Litecoin & Dogecoin's* are *Scrypt*.

Mining Contract is a method of investing in Bitcoin mining hardware, allowing anyone to rent out a pre-specified amount of hashing power for an agreed amount of time. The mining service takes care of hardware maintenance, hosting and electricity costs, making it simpler for investors.

Mining Pool is formed when a group of miners have decided to combine their computing power for mining. This allows rewards to be distributed more consistently between participants in the pool.

Mining Rig is a computer especially designed for processing proof-of-work blockchains like Ethereum. They often consist of multiple high-end graphic processors to maximize their processing power.

Minting is the process of rewarding users in proof-of-stake coins. New coins are minted as the reward for verifying transactions in a block.

Mixing Service – See 'laundry'

Mobile Wallet is a wallet which runs a 'mobile client', allowing people to have Bitcoin wallets on their phones, tablet and computers and pay on the go.

Money Laundering is the act of trying to 'clean' money earned from criminal activity by converting these profits to what appear to be legitimate assets.

Mooning in the crypto-world refers to a price going up astronomically.

Mt. Gox was a Bitcoin exchange based in Japan that collapsed in February 2014 due to poor security practices and incompetent management.

Multisig or multi-signature, refers to having more than one signature to approve a transaction. This form of security is beneficial for a company receiving money into their BTC wallet. A company may not want one employee to have sole access to a transaction so *multisig* allows for a transaction to be verified by two separate employees before it's complete. It provides an added layer of security by requiring more than one key to authorize a transaction.

N

Namecoin is an altcoin which implemented a distributed DNS (domain name system) among other features. This distributed DNS helps people using the .bit domain to resist internet censorship. It can also be used to refer to the unit of currency NMC.

Network is a peer-to-peer network that propagates transactions and blocks to every Bitcoin node on the network.

Network Effect is the increase in value of goods or a service that occurs when its use becomes more widespread.

NFC is an acronym for *Near Field Communication*, a low-power, short-range method of wireless communication. This can be used to build upon RFID systems. It was most recently implemented in the *Apple Pay* app.

Node is essentially a computer that connects to a cryptocurrency network and helps to verify the blockchain's accuracy through validation and relaying of transactions while receiving a copy of the full blockchain itself.

Nonce is a random number used once only when a miner attempts to hash a transaction block. The parameters of these numbers are set by the 'difficulty'.

O

Off Blockchain Transactions are the exchanges of value which occur off the blockchain between trusted parties. These occur because they are quicker and do not bloat the blockchain.

Open Source is the practice of sharing the source code for computer software, allowing it to be distributed and altered by anyone.

Oracles works as a bridge between the real world and the blockchain by providing data to the smart contracts.

Orphaned Block is a valid block which is discarded by the network after the blockchain has 'forked' and then re-achieved consensus on a single blockchain. This usually happens after two miners simultaneously solve a block, temporarily resulting in two valid blocks in the blockchain.

OTC or Over The Counter Exchange is an exchange where trading is done directly between the two parties involved in the transaction, allowing traders to escape some of the limitations set by trading on formalised exchanges.

Output is the part of the transaction which contains instructions for the sending of Bitcoin.

P

Paper Wallet is a form of 'cold storage' where the private keys are printed onto a piece of paper and stored offline.

Peercoin was the first cryptocurrency to implement proof-of-stake alongside proof-of-work

P2P is the acronym for *Peer-to-Peer Network*. It is the decentralization interaction between two parties or more in a highly interconnected network. Participants of a P2P network deal directly with each other through a single mediation point. Peer-to-peer has become a very large focus of blockchain as one of the biggest selling points in decentralization. Nearly every interaction on the blockchain can be fulfilled P2P, or without a centralized variable like a store, bank or notary.

Pre-mining is the mining of a cryptocurrency by its developers before it is released to the public. This can be done with good intentions, however it is also strongly associated with *scamcoins*.

Price Bubble is an economic cycle in which the price of a security or asset will surge unsustainably, and then crash as a selloff occurs. This is usually caused by speculation and has been observable in Bitcoin's past prices. When done deliberately, this is known as a *Pump and Dump*

Private Key is a secret series of letters and numbers kept by the owner of the cryptocurrency that allows access to tokens in a specific wallet and allows it to be spent by the owner. They act as passwords and should be kept secret at all times. It is also known as a secret key.

Proof-of-Burn is a method of 'burning' one proof-of-work cryptocurrency in order to receive a different cryptocurrency. This is a form of 'bootstrapping' one cryptocurrency off of another, and is done by sending coins to a verifiable and unspendable address.

Proof of Existence is a service provided through the blockchain that allows anyone to anonymously and securely store a proof-of-existence for any document they choose online. This allows people to prove that a document existed at a certain point in time and demonstrate their ownership of it, without fear of that proof being taken from them.

Proof-of-Stake is the proposed consensus algorithms to be used by Ethereum. To ensure the safety, security, incorruptibility and anonymity of cryptocurrencies being traded without the need for a centralized database or bank, there needs to be a way to prove one's work (PoW) or prove that one has a stake (PoS). Proof-of-stake has been considered the greener alternative to proof-of-work. Instead of mining in its current form, owners of ETH will be able to 'lock up' their Ether for a short period of time in order to 'vote' and generate network consensus. These stakeholders will then be rewarded with ETH by doing so.

Proof-of-Work or POW is the current consensus algorithm used by Ethereum. Proof of work was a concept originally designed to sieve spam emails and prevent DDOS attacks. A proof-of-work is essentially a datum that is very costly to produce in terms of time and resources, but can be very simply verified by another party. The proof-of-work for Bitcoin is referred to as a 'nonce', or number used only once. This has been considered an energy-intensive alternative to proof-of-stake as the computers unfortunately have to be on and running, which also drives the market towards centralization of hashing power; which is what the blockchain aims to defeat!

Public Address is the cryptographic hash of a public key. It acts as an email address that can be published anywhere; unlike private keys.

Public Key is a unique address consisting of a string of numbers and letters derived from a private key. A public key allows one to receive cryptocurrencies.

Pump and Dump is a form of market manipulation usually performed on small market cap stocks and now on cryptocurrencies. This occurs when traders artificially inflate the assets price and then exit their positions, causing a price collapse.

Q

Quantitative Easing is a form of monetary policy where a central bank purchases government securities with cash which did not exist before, in order to increase the money supply and lower interest rates.

QR code is an acronym for *Quick Response* code and is a two-dimensional barcode which can have data encoded onto it. It is a digital representation of a Bitcoin public or private key that is easy to scan by digital camera.

R

REKT is when a person has had a bad loss.

Raiden Network is an off-chain scaling solution designed to enable near-instant, low-fee and scalable payments. It is complementary to the Ethereum blockchain and works with any ERC20 compatible token. It is still a work in progress and the goal is to research state channel technology, define protocols and develop reference implementations.

Remittance is a sum of money being sent as a payment or gift.

Reward is an amount included in each new block as a reward by the network to the miner who found (solved) the proof-of-work solution.

Ripple is an alternative payment network to Bitcoin and based on similar cryptography. The Ripple network uses XRP as currency and is capable of sending any asset type.

S

Satoshi is the smallest divisible unit of one Bitcoin. There are 100 million satoshi to one Bitcoin. One satoshi equals 0.00000001 Bitcoin.

Satoshi Nakamoto is the mysterious creator of Bitcoin. Known to possess over a million Bitcoins, his/her/their identity is still unknown.

Scamcoins are coins created as get-rich-quick schemes by their developers. These coins usually have certain properties such as being clones of an existing coin and being pre-mined.

Scrypt is a type of cryptographic algorithm used by *Litecoin, Dogecoin* and many other cryptocurrencies. Compared to SHA256, this is quicker as it does not consume as much processing time.

Secret Key is also known as a private key.

Seed is the private key used in a 'deterministic wallet'

Segwit (Segregated Witness) is an improvement to the core way Bitcoin handles transactions in order to make the Bitcoin network approve more transactions with each block.

Self-Executing Contract or 'smart contract' has protocols that facilitate or enforce the obligations of a contract without the need for human intervention.

SHA256 is a specific hash function or cryptographic algorithm used by cryptocurrencies such as Bitcoin. It uses a lot of computing power and processing time and has forced miners to form mining pools to capture gains.

Sharding is a scaling solution for blockchains. Typically, every node in a blockchain network houses a complete copy of the blockchain but *sharding* allows nodes to have partial copies of the complete blockchain in order to increase overall network performance and consensus speeds.

Sidechains are theoretical, independent blockchains which are 'two-way-pegged' to the Bitcoin blockchain. These can have their own unique features and can have Bitcoins sent to and from them.

Signature is the mathematical operation that proves ownership over a wallet, coin, data etc. An example: a private key can verify with the whole network that a signature matches and a transaction is valid. The private key is only known to the owner and it is mathematically impossible to uncover.

Silk Road was the online marketplace where drugs and other illicit items could be traded for Bitcoin. Accessed through 'TOR'. Silk Road was shut down in October 2013 by the FBI.

Smart Contract is a computer protocol designed to digitally facilitate the negotiation of a contract and is enforced by the participants of the network. A two-way smart contract is an unalterable agreement stored on the blockchain that has specific logic operations akin to a real world contract. Once signed, it can never be altered. A smart contract can be used to define certain computational benchmarks or barriers that have to be met in turn for money or data to be deposited or may also be used to verify things such as land rights. It is an Ethereum-specific term.

Soft Fork is a change to the operating protocol for a cryptocurrency that is backward-compatible, so that older nodes that don't upgrade will still function. It requires most miners to upgrade in order to enforce it.

Software Wallet is storage for cryptocurrency that exists purely as software files on a computer. Software wallets can be generated for free from a variety of sources such as *MyEtherWallet*.

Solidity is one of the most popular Ethereum programming languages in which smart contracts can be written. It has some similarities to Javascript. It is an Ethereum-specific term.

Solo Miner is an individual miner working alone. The likelihood of a solo miner finding a block to pay for their equipment (computer) and electricity is so low that it constitutes a gamble (similar to playing the lottery).

SPV is an acronym for *Simplified Payment Verification* which allows mobile clients to make payments without the need for a copy of the entire blockchain.

Stable Coin is a cryptocurrency with extremely low volatility that can be used to trade against the overall market.

Stale Block is a block that has already been solved and thus cannot offer miners any reward for further work on it.

T

TA is the acronym for *Trend Analysis or Technical Analysis* and refers to the process of examining current charts in order to predict which way the market will move next.

Taint is a measure of the correlation between two addresses and is used in attempts to track a coin's history.

TCP/IP – is an acronym that stand for *Transmission Control Protocol/ Internet Protocol* and is the connection protocol used by the internet.

Testnet is a blockchain on which developers can test and experiment with changes to a cryptocurrency without the risk of damaging or interfering with the real blockchain.

The Flippening is a potential future event wherein Ethereum's market cap surpasses Bitcoin's market cap, making Ethereum the most 'valuable' crypto-currency.

Timestamp is used as proof that a piece of data existed at a certain point in time. For Bitcoin, this is the cryptographic proof of when transactions have taken place.

Token refers to new cryptocurrency created and distributed to the public through an Initial Coin Offering in order to fund a project development.

TOR refers to *The Onion Router* and is a free web browser designed to protect users' anonymity and resist censorship. It allows users to surf the web anonymously and access sites on the 'deepweb'.

Total Coin Supply. For many cryptocurrencies, there is a limit on the total number of coins that will ever come into existence. Bitcoin's total supply is capped at 21 million coins.

Transaction is an entry in the blockchain that describes a transfer from one address to another. It may contain several inputs and outputs.

Transaction Block is a group of transactions that are collected and hashed and added to the blockchain.

Transaction Fees or miners' fees, are added up to create the block reward that a miner receives when a block is successfully processed.

Turing Complete refers to the ability of a machine to perform calculations that any other programmable computer is capable of, for example an EVM.

V

Vanity Address is a Bitcoin address which contains a desired word/pattern or sequence of numbers like the personalized number plates on a car, for example: 1GEORGE2K4rWabeDmCds38ox2VXdeBE7LNd

Vault is a type of Bitcoin wallet provided by *Coinbase* that adds additional time-lock and security measures for protection of funds.

Velocity of Money is an indicator of how quickly money received is then spent again. For Bitcoin, 'Bitcoin days destroyed' is used to measure its velocity. This can indicate whether people are hoarding or spending their Bitcoins.

Venture Capitalist refers to an individual or organization that provides initial funding for start-up business ventures that cannot access public funding. This money is known as 'seed funding', and is usually exchanged for equity in the start-up.

Virgin Bitcoin is a Bitcoin that has been received by a miner as a block reward and thus has never been 'spent' before.

Vitalik Buterin is a Russian Canadian programmer who co-founded Ethereum, having written a white paper in late 2013 arguing that Bitcoin needed a scripting language for application development.

Volatility is a measure of fluctuations in price of a financial instrument over time. High volatility in Bitcoin is seen as risky since its shifting value discourages people from spending or accepting it.

W

Wallet is a storage facility for the private keys of cryptocurrencies. Each wallet allows access to view and create transactions on a specific blockchain that the wallet is designed for. It controls and allows payment of a specific amount to a specific person. There are a number of different kinds of wallets: web wallets, desktop wallets, hardware wallets, mobile wallets, paper wallets and brain wallets.

Wei is the smallest denomination of Ether. 1 Ether = 1000000000000000000 Wei (10^{18})

Whale is someone who owns an absurd amount of cryptocurrency.

Whitepaper is a report or guide made to discuss an issue or help decision-making. Satoshi Nakamoto released the whitepaper on Bitcoin, titled *Bitcoin: A Peer-to-Peer Electronic Cash System* in late 2008.

Wire Transfer is an electronic method of transferring money from one party to another.

Z

Zerocoin is a project aimed at introducing true anonymity into the Bitcoin network.

Zero Confirmation Transaction is a Bitcoin transaction that has been relayed to nodes in the Bitcoin network but has not yet been incorporated into a block. Also known as an 'unconfirmed transaction'.

Bibliography

Ashton, M., 2016. *What's Wrong with Money?: The Biggest Bubble of All.* John Wiley & Sons.

Davies, D. and Read, T., 2015. *Secret Life of Money-Everyday Economics Explained.* John Blake Publishing.

Davis, L.M., 2010. *The Facebook Era: Tapping Online Social Networks to Build Better Products, Reach New Audiences, and Sell More Stuff.*

Dunstan, B., *Understanding Finance with the Australian Financial Review* 2nd. Edition Wrightbooks.

Greenfield, S.E., 1980. *The architecture of microcomputers.* Winthrop Computer Systems Series

Mell, A. and Walker, O., 2014. *Rough Guide to Economics.* London: Rough.

Moore, S., 2015. Digital Wealth: *An Automatic Way to Invest Successfully.* John Wiley & Sons.

Romans, C., 2015. *Smart is the new rich: Money guide for millennials.* John Wiley & Sons.

Sehgal, K., 2015. Coined: *The Rich Life of Money and How Its History Has Shaped Us.* Hachette UK.

Sironi, P., 2016. *FinTech innovation: from robo-advisors to goal based investing and gamification.* John Wiley & Sons.

Tapscott, D., 2014. *The digital economy.* McGraw-Hill Education,.

Tompkins, W.J. and Webster, J.G., 1988. *Interfacing Sensors to the IBM PC* (p. 2). Upper Saddle River, NJ: Prentice Hall.

Williamson, J., 2018. *How Money Works: The Facts Visually Explained.* Reference Reviews, 32(1), pp.8-8.

Reference and copyright credits

The authors and the publisher (*Arthur Phillip Books*) have made every effort to credit and refer to the images, graphs, tables, and other statistics mentioned in this book. If any attribution is incorrect, the publisher will correct the factual and reference error(s) once it has been brought to their attention on the next print. Kindly contact the publishers at arthurphillipbooks@gmail.com.

Index of keywords

About the authors

Brian McNicol followed his father into the accounting profession and was exposed to the stock market at an early age purchasing shares in companies that his father worked for, or on recommendations from his father's stockbroking advisers. Brian dabbled in the share market for many years having a portfolio of shares ranging from *Blue Chip to Penny Dreadful*.

Over the years, Brian has spent thousands of dollars on books and hundreds of thousands of dollars on education and mentoring. He has learnt lessons, sometimes costly, to be wary of new 'gurus' with little long-term experience, new schemes that are not tested over time, and things that are too good to be true. Brian has a wealth of experience and has made mistakes along the way. Ask him about negative gearing and interest rates of 18 per cent. He has spoken at a number of large events but prefers talking to small groups or one-on-one with other investors. This book, and the others that will follow in this series, is one way that Brian can give back to the community.

Today Brian focusses mainly on commercial property both as an investor and as a buyer's agent through his company *Commercial Property Buyers Agency Australia*.

It is his enquiring mind that has driven him to look at Bitcoin and cryptocurrencies and ultimately to write this book.

Muthu Pannirselvam has had a varied international career that has included university teaching, industry consulting, strategic advising and property investment. Muthu's father was an accountant who worked in a financial institution and his mother was an economics and commerce teacher. Muthu acquired business acumen from a very young age that developed further while he helped his family business. After reaching America in his early 20s, he started to learn more about western economics and business. His knowledge on western economics has grown exponentially after his mentor in the financial world suggested that he read books like *The Wealth of Nations* where *Adam Smith* discusses labour, capital, land and technology. Now he joins hands with his mentor and co-author Brian McNicol to extend his property journey through books and coaching, mainly in the areas of commercial properties.

Muthu was always curious of knowing 'how things work' from atoms to space. His curiosity has helped him to hone his skills in research and development. He has developed products in the USA and in Australia and writes programs and codes for mobile and web applications. He is an author and an editor of various technical articles for trades-teaching, and a recent book focussed on technology and smart cities.

Commercial Property Buyers Agency

As we have suggested earlier in this book, it is important to consider taking some profits made through cryptocurrencies and invest them in some main stream investments. *Commercial Property Buyers Agency* is a boutique company specialising in the purchase of commercial property, on behalf of its clients. The company is very active in the commercial property real estate market and in regular contact with many commercial real estate agents.

We will, as a buyer's agent, always work in the best interest of the client, and always look to secure a property at the lowest possible price and best terms. We understand time and budget constraints and will work within those to secure a property at a price and terms favourable to the client.

Our aim is to purchase a commercial property that meets our client's requirements, will attract and retain quality tenants, have good long-term leases and provide strong rental yield. Above all, we aim to save our clients time, money and stress. We are committed to always acting with integrity and honesty and in our client's best interest. If you would like to find out more about how *Commercial Property Buyers Agency* can find the right commercial property for you, or more about mentoring, contact cpbuyersagency@gmail.com. Visit our website www.cpbuyersagency.com

Other Books by the Authors

We hope that you have found the information in this book useful. If you have any questions, or if you would like to provide a testimonial, please email us at arthurphillipbooks@gmail.com.

Arthur Phillip Books is publishing six books in the next 12 months under the series title, *"It's My Time".*

A key to success is to continually improve your financial competence and this series of books is designed to assist with improving your competency in property investment.

The first book in this series is titled *'It's My Time: The A to Z of Property and Financial Terms'*. It was designed as a resource, a useful reference for terminology, providing reference websites and some basic forms. It is designed to complement our next books in the series.

The second book titled *'It's My Time: Setting Financial and Personal Goals'* is about planning and developing a blueprint for the rest of your life, regardless of your age. Most people have no financial plan, nor a belief that they can be financially free. Many invest in shares and/or property with little thought as to why they are doing so, or how it will fit into their current or future, lifestyle.

The third book in the series is titled *'It's My Time: Successful Residential Investing'* then builds upon the first two and focusses on residential property investment. We will delve into aspects of being a landlord that aren't included in most books, for example abandoned goods and meth labs.

The fourth book titled *'It's My Time: Introducing Commercial Investing'* is about commercial real estate. Commercial real estate in the last couple of years has seen an increase in popularity as the yield from residential property declines. Many SMSFs are also looking at commercial property because of the returns and the long-term leases.

'It's My Time: Planning a Holistic Retirement' is the fifth book in this series. This book covers planning for retirement: not only financially but also how to transition from work life to retirement – where you may live, friendships outside of work, and what you will do to fill in your day without going to work: travel, volunteering, part time work, etc.

'It's My Time: Strategies in Action' is the sixth book in this series. This book is about planning and developing a blueprint for the rest of your life, regardless of your age. It is about taking what you have learnt in the other books and creating a strategy. One of the important things with establishing your strategy is that you follow your strategy, and repeat it, and keep repeating it. This is the secret to financial success: becoming a master at those things that make up your strategy and staying focused.

All pre-ordered books or additional copies purchased through our website receive a 10% discount off the listed price. If you would like to pre-order any of these books, visit our website www.arthurphillipbooks.com or email us at arthurphillipbooks@gmail.com. or contact us on +61-451-902-123.